The Age of Myths & Legends

—

Book One: Monsters

T.D. Hill

Sky Lodge Publishing

DAYTON, OHIO

Copyright © 2017 by Terrell Hill

All rights reserved. No part of this publication may be reproduced, distributed or transmitted in any form or by any means, without prior written permission.

T. D. Hill/Sky Lodge Publishing
2312 Far Hills Ave. #342
Dayton, Ohio/45419
www.nativetales.com

Library of Congress Control Number: 2017909553

The Age of Myths and Legends/ T.D. Hill. -- 1st ed.
ISBN 978-0-692-81991-3

Dedicated to my grandfather, Donald Horsechief, one of the greatest warriors I've ever known.

Contents

Preface 5
The Old World 7
Lords of the Earth 13
Terrors of the Deep 28
Masters of Wood and Water 48
Denizens of the Dark 63
Servants of Evil 81
Gratitude 99
Bibliography 100
About the Author 102

Proem

Preface

If you can believe it, this book actually came about by accident. In college, I was once given an interesting assignment by my Sociology professor, Dr. Garcia. For this project, I was supposed to interview a first generation immigrant family in the Rio Grande Valley. We were to discuss the challenges that these families faced while trying to assimilate into mainstream American culture. However, my professor suggested that I should interview my own grandparents instead. I was more than a little skeptical of his suggestion, because my grandparents weren't immigrants. Actually, they were members of the first group of Americans. My grandmother was a full-blooded member of the Kiowa Tribe of Oklahoma, and my grandfather was an enrolled member of the Wichita and Affiliated Tribes of Oklahoma. He was a member of the Pawnee Nation of Oklahoma as well.

However, I soon came to realize that many of the trials and tribulations that immigrant families faced were parallel to the hardships that Native American families had sought to overcome as well. I decided to take my professor's advice.

During Spring Break of that year, I returned to Southwestern Oklahoma to interview my grandparents for my Sociology project. It sounds so cliché, but it truly was an eye-opening experience. They shared stories with me about our family and our culture that I had never heard before. My grandfather explained the importance of song and storytelling. My grandmother shared old Kiowa songs and stories that were told to her when she was a little girl. On that day, I felt a deep sense of connection to my people, and I wanted to preserve these stories for our family. As I grew older and had the opportunity to travel across the country, I began to record stories from other tribes. The more stories I recorded, the more similarities I began to see in our various tribal cultures. Eventually, I decided to put these stories down on paper in a more cohesive format. This step marked the beginning of my first manuscript for the Age of Myths and Legends.

It is my hope that you, the reader, will come away from this reading with an appreciation for the power, wisdom, and grace of these timeless myths and legends. Most importantly, I hope that you will share these stories with your friends, with your family, and even with strangers. Once you read (or hear) the old stories, you, too, will become a caretaker of these tales, and with every telling we all breathe new life into these wonderful stories.

Austin, TX., October, 2016   T.D. Hill

Introduction

The Old World

INTRODUCTION

The Old World

"And hence arose the host of miscreants,
Monsters and elves and eldritch sprites,
Warlocks and giants, that warred against God;
Jotuns and Goblins; He gave them their due."
Beowulf

The old world...it was a lost age between myth and memory. It was the time when the rich, verdant forest of the land stretched from sea to sea. The majestic mountains cloaked in snow and mists were still virgin and untrodden by Man. The restless oceans and endless skies were still replete with mystery and wonder. This was a world that was utterly alien yet strangely familiar, full of mystery, miracle, and magic. In this lost age, Man, Beast, Bird, and Tree still spoke one tongue. Each interacted in each other's lives daily. The winding rivers, deep valleys, and ethereal clouds above were sentient as well, infused with the potent life force of the Earth itself.

So young was the world in this first epoch that even the firmaments of the heavens were yet to be established. Nevertheless, an order, meaning, and truth existed even then in this forgotten age, when things were less known but, perhaps, better understood.

Amongst these universal truths known by early Man was the ephemeral concept of the Dark. Since the beginning, Man had always feared the darkness, because it was the one element in which the gift of sight was useless. That fact, along with early Man's observations of the natural world, only served to fuel his belief that there was something sinister and esoteric about the shadows and the night.

Early Man observed how the prairie dog of the western plains knew innately that shadows and silhouettes in the darkening skies above spelt doom. Forest animals took to the high tree tops or deep subterranean abodes when the sun set, and the shadows lengthened. Smaller animals were born knowing that owls, bears, mountain lions, and wolves prowled the nighttime landscape in search of prey.

In that long ago age, Man knew that dwelling in large groups afforded better protection. He also knew that fire and light were wards against the encroaching darkness and could keep the wild animals of the night at bay.

Man also knew that in the lonely places of the world, in darkling woods, in homeless hills, and out of the depths of the very Earth itself, baleful beings of a much darker order crept forth into the night.

The forms and appearances of these maleficent beings were almost as countless as the stars above. Some took on the shapes of great beasts and serpents, spilling blood upon the earth with claw and fang. Others took no corporeal form at all and instead became sinister spirits against which there was little defense. The worst of these beings, perhaps, were those who masqueraded in human guise while spreading sickness and disease amongst man, woman, and child.

Many have wondered where these dark beings of the shadows came from. No one knew for certain, not even the Wise. However, a multitude of old tales from the many tribes of North America sought to answer such a question. In the earliest of Navajo myths, it was said that monsters were sent unto this world from the Lower World, out of spite, by the First Man and First Woman, Atse Hastiin and Atse Asdzan. For the early Wichita and Affiliated Tribes of the Southern plains, it was believed that monsters served as foreboding harbingers of impending world destruction. It was thought that such creatures were destined to appear at the end of every Earthly cycle.

For many tribes of the Northwest coast, it was believed that ghosts and other supernatural beings had always dwelt with Man, ever since the Primordial Darkness had first lain upon the face of the Earth. Among the Yamasee and Cherokee nations of the Southeast there exists the haunting tale of Ocasta the Stone-Coat, who was to become the bane of the living world and a paragon of utter wickedness. This being was likely the greatest of the first evils ever to exist, as he was considered the father of so many of the world's malignant ills.

In that age, so long ago, when the moon that brightened the night sky was yet unstained, the Creator of the Universe looked down upon his struggling creations and pitied their sorrowful plight. Man had yet to reach his full stature and lived little better than the beasts of the fields, so the Creator sent unto them a mighty spirit of wisdom and power named Ocasta.

Ocasta was a bearer of great and other worldly knowledge. Under his tutelage, Early Man prospered. The wide fields yielded bountiful harvest with the introduction of seeds and tools provided by Ocasta. The great forests surrendered their secrets, providing edible roots and curative herbs. Men no longer huddled in cold, dark caves but were taught to build homes and shelters using the natural materials of the Earth. In time, Man came to live in a veritable Golden Age full of peace and prosperity made wholly possible by the wise counsel of the mighty spirit.

However, it came to pass that Ocasta spent less and less time amongst men. Instead, he spent his days in solitude, withholding his sage teachings.

As the months slowly melted away into years, it appeared to mortal men that the countenance of the wise and gentle spirit had grown cold. They could not know that their benefactor and mentor wrestled with dark thoughts utterly alien to his native nature.

Though Ocasta was a demiurgic being, he became lost in his own spiritual darkness and was consumed by jealousy. "Why should Man be afforded all of the Creator's love and grace? Man is but the weakest being in all of Creation. What is he but a blight upon the lands?" he thought to himself.

In an act of calculated blasphemy, Ocasta began to lead naive Man astray with evil rites and ceremonies. With these wicked acts, the mighty spirit introduced dark forbidden knowledge into the hearts and minds of men and women. Through Ocasta's actions, the very first witches were brought forth unto an unsuspecting world.

Not content with this lone act of evil, Ocasta then used his vast thaumaturgy to corrupt the beasts of the fields and forest. The once peaceful creatures of the wild grew sharp fangs and deadly claws. The cold yet benign serpents and reptiles of the great waterways grew far larger and stronger than their erstwhile cousins. Through Ocasta's evil will, blood-thirsty monsters that preyed upon both Man and Beast now haunted the dark places. The Golden Age of Man had come to a close with the introduction of Ocasta's wicked corruptions, and, for a while, all men and virtuous beasts were hard-pressed by these abominations. Many came to believe that Man would not survive the coming ages.

Over time, though, a curious thing began to happen to Man. Ingenuity and necessity, the progeny of desperation, had at last begun to open new avenues of thought for Early Man. Though he still feared the dark and its horrible new denizens, Man had learned to defend his own with prayer, with fire, and with a wondrous new weapon: the bow and arrow.

At times, Ocasta would travel invisible and unclad from village to village, leaving chaos and civil unrest in his wake. On one such travel, Ocasta chanced upon a solitary man hunting in the forest. The hunter carried a strange new instrument on his back. Ocasta was intrigued, so he followed the hunter deeper into the woods.

The hunter, perhaps sensing the foul presence of the dark spirit, stopped and surveyed his surroundings. He saw nothing. Human senses are ill-equipped to deal with beings of such power, so the hunter continued on. Soon, the hunter spotted a deer. He carefully aimed his weapon and fired. Ocasta was utterly shocked to see the deer fall to the ground, pierced by the marvelous new weapon, the arrow. While the hunter offered thanks and prayer for his successful hunt, Ocasta carefully examined the arrow and its flint tip.

For the first time in ages upon ages, fear had gripped the spirit's heart. While it was true that he was a spiritual being of great power, he could still be slain while on this mortal coil. Therefore, Ocasta spent many months wandering the lands, gathering bits and pieces of flint as he went. When he had amassed a great number, he placed the flint pieces on the ground and called upon his mighty thaumaturgy. Through his power, he crafted the flint pieces into a powerful coat of armor. Upon donning this coat, he deemed himself invincible. He then waged open war upon mankind and his dwellings. He mercilessly pillaged villages and spilt the blood of innocents to feast upon their hearts and livers.

The Lord of Darkness

As the months slowly melted away into years, it appeared to mortal men that the countenance of the wise and gentle spirit had grown cold. They could not know that their benefactor and mentor wrestled with dark thoughts utterly alien to his native nature.

Brave warriors attempted to fight back with bow and spear, but it was to no avail. Many lost their lives attempting to defend their people. The only recourse left for many villagers was to flee upon Ocasta's approach, but even then there was no escape from Ocasta, now known as the Stone-Coat. With his staff of magic, he could follow mortals anywhere. When thrown into the air, the staff would transform into a stone bridge, which Ocasta used to cross deep ravines and rivers.

In desperation, the villagers turned to their holy men. These wise men of lore had learned to interpret dreams, heal the sick, and banish evil spirits. The hierophants told the villagers that the only way to assault the Stone-Coat was to place seven undressed, moon-sick women in his path at set intervals.

Seven such women were found, and each was made to lie in the path of the demon as he approached the village. When he reached the first woman, Ocasta scornfully reproached her, "Heya! You should be ashamed to be seen in such a way!"

In disgust, he left her where she lay, but he was sickened and somewhat weakened after this encounter. He approached the second woman in his path and suffered the same results. As he passed each consecutive woman, he grew weaker and weaker until, at last, upon encountering the seventh woman, he fell to the earth vomiting blood.

As quick as lightning, the seventh woman leapt up and pulled back a piece of Ocasta's stone coat. With all of her mortal might, she drove a stake of basswood deep into his heart. The scream of agony that issued forth from Ocasta's lips shook the foundations of the world. Mighty trees were uprooted, the mountains shuddered, and the great waters hissed and boiled.

Though he withered in agony, Ocasta did not die. When the villagers saw this, they quickly gathered basswood and set the mortally wounded Ocasta ablaze.

As the flames consumed the demiurgic being, Ocasta felt no ill will towards Man. He looked upon the villagers with wonder and admiration. "How far Man has come from the timid creature that he once was," thought Ocasta. "Surely one day he will hold dominion over the world."

Ocasta called out to the villagers and begged them to listen well to his words and learn as best they could. As the fires greedily consumed his body, Ocasta began to sing songs of power. He sang songs of healing and songs of wisdom. He sang songs of war and songs of the harvest and of peace.

The villagers learned all they could until Ocasta sang no more. When the mighty fires of the pyre had died down to nothing more than red embers, the villagers raked the ashes and discovered a lump of Red Wadi paint. This paint became sacred to them, and it was reserved for use in prayer and ceremonies.

At last, a great evil was forever banished from the world of Men. Even though he had wrought much wickedness unto the world, Ocasta had also left a means with which to combat the Dark and its terrible denizens: prayer and, most importantly, hope. In truth, Man would most certainly need these potent tools, for the night was still very young.

Chapter One

Lords of the Earth

CHAPTER ONE

Lords of the Earth

There were Giants in the Earth in those days;"
Genesis 6:4

If the old tales speak true, a very ancient and powerful race once strode about the lands inspiring fear and awe in all who beheld them. Their size and strength were legendary and, in those days, it was not uncommon to hear wondrous tales of these beings uprooting trees, felling mountains, or spilling the wide seas. These creatures belonged to the mighty race of giants, the preternatural sons and daughters of the Earth, and the keepers of her many secrets.

As living embodiments of the Earth's destructive power, these beings were masters of magic and bearers of ancient wisdom and lore. Many could even change their size and shape if it suited their needs. Giants also had the ability to hide their hearts in different parts of their bodies. This made giants extremely hard to kill. While it is true that some used their impressive capabilities to serve as guardians and mentors to the lesser folk, most giant-kin devoted their sheer strength and vast size unto the service of evil.

Long ago, in the land of the Tlingit, one such giant terrorized the countryside and its people. The savagery of this fearsome creature of the first age was such that many brave and noble warriors would drop their weapons and tremble in terror as this massive behemoth approached. With unbridled fury, this cruel giant would tear his victims apart with teeth and claws to slake his ravenous thirst for human blood. At other times, he would take his fallen prey back to his tent nestled somewhere deep in the mountains. There, he would leisurely enjoy his gruesome feast with his monstrous young son.

In time, the Tlingit called forth a great council to discuss ways of ridding themselves of this horrifying menace. At this great meeting, ideas were proposed, strategies were exchanged, and plans were theorized. However, with so many strong-willed leaders and warriors in one place, tempers soon flared, and arguments erupted. Amidst the shouts, curses, and veiled threats that filled the evening air, one man distinguished himself from his fellows by sitting quietly in the shadows, deep in thought.

The Lone Warrior

As he strode purposefully to the forefront of the gathering, every speaker grew silent, for this was a man of great renown, a mighty warrior of the Tlingit nation. As a man of few words, he shocked the council by stating that he would kill the monster alone and unaided.

He listened intently to every speaker and measured their words carefully before he finally rose to his feet. As he strode purposefully to the forefront of the gathering, every speaker grew silent, for this was a man of great renown, a mighty warrior of the Tlingit nation. As a man of few words, he shocked the council by stating that he would kill the monster alone and unaided. With that, he left the stunned gathering and went to the location where the giant was known to haunt.

The warrior hid his weapons in the bushes and laid down onto the soft grass, feigning death. His wait was not long, for out of the gloom strode the giant. Perplexed, the giant approached the prostrate warrior cautiously. He carefully poked and prodded the hero, and, when the mortal did not respond, the giant laughed in his throat, "What a fine meal this one will make, and he's still warm."

The giant picked up the seemingly lifeless warrior and carried him back to his tent deep in the mountains. Once home, he dropped the warrior near the cooking pit, but there was no wood with which to build a cooking fire. Cursing and grumbling to himself, the angry giant stomped out of his tent and into the growing darkness.

The warrior, though bruised and battered, sprang to life and surveyed his surroundings. He spotted a large knife and grabbed it just moments before the giant's son entered the tent. Before the young giant could react, the warrior leapt onto his chest and held the sharp knife to his throat. "Now tell me where your father's heart is!" threatened the warrior. The young giant whimpered hoarsely, "In his left heel."

The warrior quickly dispatched the young giant and stealthily waited by the tent entrance. As before, the warrior's wait was not long, for he soon heard the giant's heavy footsteps thudding in the distance. The warrior's heart raced with anticipation. Every second seemed an eternity, and beads of sweat covered his brow. The Tlingit warrior could barely contain himself until, finally, the fearsome giant ducked his head into the tent.

The hero steeled his resolve and courage and, in a wild leap, threw himself at the giant. With all of the warrior's earthly might, he drove the sharp blade deep into the monster's heel. The giant, screaming in rage and despair, fell backwards out of the tent. His fall was so fierce that it shook the very foundations of the mountains themselves.

The Tlingit hero grimly watched as the giant kicked and convulsed in the dusk. Finally, the giant lay still, and the hero carefully approached. In a blur of movement, the giant suddenly turned and fixed the hero with a malevolent gaze and smiled, "Though I shall soon die, it shall not stop me from drinking the blood of your race forever."

The malicious spark of life finally faded from the giant's eyes, and his chest labored no more. The mortal hero pondered the giant's last threat and decided to burn the monster's body to ash to ensure its death. He labored long and hard to gather enough wood and, at first, had difficulty starting the fire. With determination, he set the giant's body ablaze. The funeral pyre burned brightly throughout the night, greedily consuming the monster's corpse. When morning came, all that remained of the giant was a large heap of gray ash. The warrior gathered the ashes and threw them into the air for the four winds to scatter.

Alas, to his horror, the cloud of ash became a cloud of mosquitoes, and, in the distance, the warrior heard the giant's cold laughter echoing among the hills. "I shall still continue to drink the blood of your race forever."

Giants loomed large in nearly all of the ancient stories of the Indigenous tribes of North America. There are some tales that speak of gentle giants, like Koodlowetto of the Inuit, who were much more interested in hunting beasts than men. These few gentle giants could even be considered benevolent.

Yet, in most of the old tales, giants wrought terrible havoc and destruction all across the land. In order for Man and Beast to survive the coming ages, these giants had to be brought low. Needless to say, this was a daunting task. Giants were perhaps the living embodiments of the Earth's power; nevertheless, they were still cloaked in mortality and, most importantly, could be slain. The Zia told tales of the great heroes, Ma'asewe and Uyuuyewe, who once killed a member of a wicked and powerful race of giants called the Sko'yo. In tales of the Ojibwa, the Powers that Be once sent one hundred winged men, who brought down a giant said to be so powerful that he might have consumed the entire world.

In many tales, like those told by the Tlingit, giants were brought low by mortal heroes who braved these monsters' tremendous strength and infernal powers armed with little more than faith and dauntless courage. However, such heroes were few and far between. For this reason, many native peoples sought to avoid the destructive giants altogether, if they could. Certain places of the old world, such as mountains and lakes, were generally avoided due to the inherently chaotic power of natural forces, such as rapids, waterfalls, and rockslides. Fittingly, many giants, as chaotic creatures themselves, were attracted to the primal, anarchic aura of these natural environments, and they made these places their homes.

There were many tribal cultures who acknowledged the association between the dangers of certain natural locations and the giants who inhabited them. The Washoe tribe avoided the craggy, windswept mountains of Nevada, particularly Pine Nut Mountain. This rocky height was home to a cunning, one-eyed giant who preyed upon any who trespassed near his cave. In the Yosemite Valley, the Southern Miwok feared the Merced River, for it was the favorite haunt of the man-eating ogre, Uwulin. Upon that river's shoreline, this giant would gut and skin his helpless victims on the nearby slabs of granite. It was once said that so much blood was spilt that some of the granite stones in the area are still stained red to this very day. To the Athabaskan-speaking tribes of the North, the rich, dense forests were sacred places to be both respected and feared. In these mysterious woods dwelt the Nakhani, a fearsome giant completely covered with coarse hair. This monster hid near summer camps so that it could suddenly spring upon and eat the unwary.

While the aforementioned giants were all male, female giants were featured in many of the old tales as well, and they were just as formidable as their male counterparts. The Central Inuit dreaded the fearsome giantess, Amayersuk. Like most giants, she enjoyed the taste of human flesh, her favorite being that of young children.

The Gentle Giant

There are some tales that speak of gentle giants, like Koodlowetto of the Inuit, who were much more interested in hunting beasts than men. These few gentle giants could even be considered benevolent.

Face The Sko'yo

The Zia told tales of the great heroes, Ma'asewe and Uyuuyewe, who once killed a member of a wicked and powerful race of giants called the Sko'yo.

Confrontation

The Washoe tribe avoided the craggy, windswept mountains of Nevada, particularly Pine Nut Mountain. This rocky height was home to a cunning, one-eyed giant who preyed upon any who trespassed near his cave.

Uwulin Colossus

In the Yosemite Valley, the Southern Miwok feared the Merced River, for it was the favorite haunt of the man-eating ogre, Uwulin. Upon that river's shoreline, this giant would gut and skin his helpless victims on the nearby slabs of granite. It was once said that so much blood was spilt that some of the granite stones in the area are still stained red to this very day.

Forest Encounter

In these mysterious woods dwelt the Nakhani, a fearsome giant completely covered with coarse hair. This monster hid near summer camps so that it could suddenly spring upon and eat the unwary.

Ambush

In the frozen North, the Inuit told tales of the giant wolf, Amarok. Much more than a large wolf, the Amarok was instead a raw being of the first age. As such, it was one of the great powers of the tundra. To dishonor this powerful being was perilous, as was hunting alone in the frozen lands under its power.

The Kwakiutl and the Salish tribes told tales of Dzunukwa, the dreaded Basket Woman. This powerful giantess carried a basket which she used to catch naughty children. Once in her lair, she would make meals out of her unfortunate captives.

Some giants who plagued mankind were not humanoid in form at all. In the frozen North, the Inuit told tales of the giant wolf, Amarok. Much more than a large wolf, the Amarok was instead a raw being of the First Age. As such, it was one of the great powers of the tundra. To dishonor this powerful being was perilous, as was hunting alone in the frozen lands under its power. However, there were always those who risked such danger for a bountiful hunt. When these hunters did not return home, it was believed that they had been taken by the Amarok.

Giants also figured prominently in the old tales told by tribes of the Iroquois Confederacy. However, these giants differed from their counterparts in the South and West. This particular race of giant had skin as hard as stone, so the Onondaga named them Ot-ne-yar-hod, meaning "Stone Giant." Stone Giants were great fishermen and hunters, but they also craved the taste of human flesh. Fortunately, for all their formidable might and strength, these giants were none too bright.

In one Oneida tale, a fearsome Stone Giant was tricked into falling off of a large cliff. In another tale, a giant was cleverly convinced that it was a much farther distance than he thought to a particular village that he intended to destroy. Perhaps the most popular story concerning a Stone Giant is the tale of the clever, yet comical, mortal named Skunny Wundy and his encounter with one of these fearsome beings.

One bright morning, when the world was still young, the braggart Skunny Wundy was busy burning the morning hours away with tales of his great courage and daring. Most of his listeners smiled and winked at each other, for they knew Skunny Wundy to be a fabulist- but what a wonderful fabulist. He could spin such entertaining webs of fantasy and mystery that most people would stop in the middle of their daily chores just to listen.
"He is a dreamer," some said. "Let him dream. He isn't hurting anybody."

All of the people in the village felt this way, and they held a special place in their hearts for him-all, that is, except for one man. The Hoya'nê, the most powerful man in the village, held very little love or respect for the storyteller. As a man of responsibility, he felt that an individual should be held accountable for his words and actions. For this reason, his mood soured when snatches of Skunny Wundy's false exploits came to his ears.

On this particular morning, the Hoya'nê had decided to take a brisk stroll and breathe in the fine morning air. His countenance grew dark, however, when he caught a glimpse of a large crowd gathered around the young storyteller. He strode up to the gathering just in time to hear a child ask, "Skunny Wundy, what would you do if you saw a Stone Giant?" The fabricator merely smiled and replied haughtily, "Why, I would break every bone in the giant's body! I would tear off his arms and legs!" The children in the audience gasped in awe as Skunny Wundy continued, "The Stone Giants fear me. Just one mention of my name would cause them to flee in terror!"

The Hoya'nê turned away in disgust as the audience cheered for the posturing young storyteller. His morning walk ruined, the Hoya'nê decided to return to his dwelling when a hunter suddenly sprinted in his direction. "Sir!" panted the hunter. "There is a Stone Giant on the other side of the river! We must warn everyone!" The Hoya'nê caught the hunter by the shoulder and whispered, "Wait!" A devious plan, one that would either expose Skunny Wundy as a liar or finish off the troublesome youth once and for all, had taken shape in the chief's mind.

With a devious smile, the Hoya'nê whispered new instructions to the frightened hunter. Then, with a purposeful stride, the tribal leader returned to the storyteller and his gathering. "Skunny Wundy," he called. "I've heard that you are one of the bravest men in the entire village. Is this true?" The young man merely smiled and nodded, so the chief continued. "I've also heard that the eaters of men, the Stone Giants, simply flee in terror at the merest mention of your name. Is this true also?" Skunny Wundy answered gravely, "It is true, honorable leader. The monsters of the world flee from my wrath and power." "Well," smiled the Hoya'nê. "I am glad to hear this. For at this very moment, there is a large Stone Giant on the other side of the river." A large gasp of fear and astonishment escaped from the crowd as the chief continued. "I have sent word to the monster that we will not flee from his might this time, because the great Skunny Wundy lives in this village, and he has sworn to slay any Stone Giant that ventures too close." The young man stifled a cry of terror as the Hoya'nê, relishing the moment, continued, "I have sent word that you will meet him at the river to do battle. I hope that the giant has sung his death song today, eh Skunny Wundy?"

The young man smiled grimly and answered bravely, "Of course I will go to the river right now to finish off this menace." A great cheer erupted from the crowd as Skunny Wundy strode towards the river. Once out of sight, the young man leaned against a tree and sobbed. He cursed himself for letting his imagination run wild and for telling so many tales.

When he had regained his composure, he crept on hands and knees to the river. He silently prayed that the giant had lost interest and left the area. To his disappointment and horror, the Stone Giant was still on the other side of the river, impatiently waiting.

Every story that Skunny Wundy had ever heard about Stone Giants appeared to be true. This monster was a being of rough and crude features, and his skin was the color of granite. The giant stood as tall as a pine tree and was as wide as a longhouse. The frightened young man wondered if it was also true that these fearsome creatures truly had the magic of the old world in their veins. Could they really hear a blade of grass growing in the underbrush? Could they truly see a grasshopper creeping through the fields a mile away?

As Skunny Wundy pondered these thoughts, he suddenly noticed the giant's jade eyes burning in the gloom. "Who's that hiding in the thicket?" called the giant, in a voice so deep and gruff that it seemed to have come from the very depths of the Earth itself. "Is it you, Skunny Wundy? Are you the one amongst mortals who can kill giants? Come out and face me!" Skunny Wundy stood up out of the underbrush and defiantly answered, "Aye! I am the great Skunny Wundy. Come across the river so that I can tear off your arms and beat you to death with them."

Challenge Accepted

This monster was a being of rough and crude features, and his skin was the color of granite. The giant stood as tall as a pine tree and was as wide as a longhouse. The frightened young man wondered if it was also true that these fearsome creatures truly had the magic of the old world in their veins.

Enraged, the Stone Giant crashed through the trees and plunged into the water. Now it just so happened that the river was fairly shallow, except for the section of the river that the giant was crossing. It was exceedingly deep, and the giant was soon lost to sight.

Skunny Wundy quickly splashed across the river to the other side. When the giant finally emerged on the other side of the river and saw the mortal man on the opposite bank, he scornfully called, "What are you doing on that side of the river? Why did you move?" Skunny Wundy shrugged his shoulders. "What are you talking about? I haven't moved. You must have gotten turned around under the water."

The giant scratched his head then shambled into the water until the river covered his gray crown. Once again, Skunny Wundy splashed across the river to the other side. The giant arose from the river ready to do battle but was flustered to see the little challenger on the opposite side of the water. "What are you doing?" called the young storyteller. "Hurry up! I haven't got all day! Besides, it's getting hot."

With a sigh, the giant plunged into the river once more, determined to crush his opposition. Once more, Skunny Wundy raced across to the other side. This time, in his haste to cross the river, he accidentally dropped his axe.

When the giant climbed out of the river, he spotted the axe sparkling in the sunlight and stooped down to pick it up. Skunny Wundy watched as the giant laughed in his throat and roared, "What's this? Is it a toy?" The giant then touched the axe blade to the tip of his tongue to test its sharpness. He then absently tossed the axe at an outcrop of boulders.

To both the giant's and Skunny Wundy's astonishment, the axe split the boulders asunder in a shower of sparks and rock fragments. The quick-thinking storyteller realized that the old tales were true; a Stone Giant truly had the magic of the old world flowing in its veins and could indeed infuse a portion of the old world magic into certain objects. The axe had now become enchanted and was capable of wondrous feats. To the slow thinking giant, it seemed as if the axe was but a reflection of its owner's might, and the monster suddenly grew very afraid. "Skunny Wundy," The giant called out nervously. "Your medicine must be great, and I do not wish to fight you. Let us part in peace." The young man recovered his wits quickly and answered defiantly, "All right giant, but know this: if you or any of your kind come anywhere near my village again, I will destroy the entire race of giants! Understand?"

"Yes!" cried the giant in terror. With that, the Stone Giant raced away into fading sunlight and was never seen or heard from again. As for Skunny Wundy, he crossed the river to return to the village and entered into the magical world of myth and legend, forever to be known as the braggart who had bested a fearsome giant of the old world.

Chapter Two

Terrors of the Deep

CHAPTER TWO

Terrors of the Deep

Hast thou entered into the springs of the sea?
Or hast thou walked in the recesses of the deep?
Have the gates of death been revealed unto thee,
Or hast thou seen the gates of the shadow of death?
Job 38:16-17

Man has always felt a certain affinity for the seas, lakes, rivers, and streams that cover most of the Earth. According to some tales from the elder days, the longing and loneliness that man feels for the waters are due to the fact that Man came from the primordial depths himself. The early people of North America acknowledged water as the bringer of life, and most tribes felt a certain sense of awe and wonderment for this powerful driving force of nature.

Like the great forest-cloaked hills and towering mountains, the waters of the old world held many mysteries to be both respected and, in some cases, feared. In those days, mysterious powers were ever-present in the wide seas and meandering rivers. Sinister spirits dwelt near roaring waterfalls and turbulent whirlpools. Even the quiet lakes and dark, stilled pools held nameless terrors lying in wait for the foolish or unwary.

One such fearsome terror of the deep waters was the dreaded horned serpent, the Uktena. These creatures haunted the lakes and streams of the Southeast and preyed upon all living things that wandered too close to their watery lairs. The Uktena were old, perhaps as old as the making of the world itself, and their strength was colossal. It was said that these mighty beasts were able to smash boulders and splinter trees with their powerful tails. It was also said that the Uktena could scar and rend the very mountains themselves with the great horns or antlers that grew from their scaly heads.

However, it was a flashing jewel embedded deep within these creatures' skulls that caught the attention of any mortal unlucky enough to encounter these monsters. This gem, called the Ulun'suti, was an item of great power and magic. In the hands of the Wise, the jewel was capable of wondrous miracles, such as the healing of the sick, the summoning of rain, the gift of fertility, and the power of prophecy. Acquiring the magical jewel from the wicked Uktena was another matter altogether. The malevolent eyes of the Uktena could paralyze its victims, and the creature possessed the ability to spit a corrosive poison over a great distance.

So infected with evil was this creature that even the environment in which it lived became barren. The vegetation near its lair turned brown and brittle, and the waterways turned black and deadly even to the touch. However, these monsters of the old world did have a weakness. Along these creatures' sinuous bodies lay numerous bands of color. Behind the seventh band of color beat these creatures' black hearts. If these organs could be pierced, the Uktena would die. In one tale of the Cherokee, this critical knowledge was put to use, not by the Cherokee themselves, but by one of that tribe's deadliest enemies, the magician, Aganunitsi.

It happened once, in olden times, that the Cherokee were at war with the powerful Shawano. The Shawano, or Shawnee, as they were to be later known, were the deadliest of adversaries, because they fought not only with conventional weapons but also with great songs of destructive power. Among these people well-versed in thaumaturgy lived Aganunitsi, mighty in the lore of his people and, perhaps, the greatest Didanawisgi of his age.

His knowledge was so vast that he knew the name and nature of every living thing that dwelt upon the Earth. A host of powerful spirits, bound to his will, waited at his beck and call, ready to do his bidding. So great were his songs of power that he could bring forth terrible storms and even summon raging fires to plague his foes.

Falsely content with his magical prowess, Aganunitsi grew complacent and reckoned little of the Cherokee's mastery of the art of subterfuge and warfare. Against all odds, this most powerful of the Wise was captured, bound, and whisked away to a Cherokee encampment. It must be said that the Cherokee were not a cruel people, but they had suffered much at the hands of Aganunitsi. The Didanawisgi was now bound to a stake, and the people of the encampment had every intention of burning him alive. Yet in that hour, so elegant and passionate were the hierophant's pleas that the Cherokee had no choice but to listen to his words and carefully consider his bold proposition.

"Release me, kind people." He pleaded. "I know that your people have suffered greatly. Your crops do not grow. The hunt is unsuccessful, and your warriors have suffered bad luck on the field of battle. Release me, and I will give your people succor. In exchange for my life, I will bring you the flashing jewel of the Uktena itself!"

The Cherokee gazed in wonder at their captured foe. Could the medicine-man really acquire the flashing jewel? Though their prisoner's power was great, the Uktena was a dark creature from the old world; surely the hierophant was mad.

However, if Aganunitsi was somehow successful, then the reward would be more than substantial. After much deliberation, the captors agreed to release the mighty Aganunitsi in exchange for the powerful jewel. The Cherokee then bound him with oaths that could not be easily broken, and he was set free.

The Didanawisgi made his way to the Smoky Mountains, where few people dwelt. On his journey, he overcame harsh terrain and suffered many hardships. Aganunitsi noted that, as he traveled farther and farther south, the creatures of the forest grew strange and dangerous. That observation, along with his supernatural senses, told him that he drew nearer to his quarry every day.

When Aganunitsi had reached the Gahuti Mountain, he knew that he had discovered the monster's abode. The trees had grown dark and twisted, corrupted by the Uktena's influence. Grass and shrubbery were dead and had given way to fungi and mold. The smell of decay and waste permeated the air and caused the Didanawisgi to gag. Every so often, as he ascended the mountain, he would spot the sun-bleached bones of some unlucky hero who had sought to contend with the dreadful Uktena.

With an arrow already knocked in his bow, Aganunitsi was cautiously making his way around an outcrop of decaying brush when he suddenly stumbled upon the Uktena. As accustomed as the hierophant was to seeing and dealing with the supernatural, he was totally unprepared for the creature's appearance and was awestruck.

The Uktena lay fast asleep on a prominence of granite that overlooked the bleak landscape. Scales the color of polished bronze covered its sinewy body. Horns, so regal and imposing that they seemed to rake the clouds above, grew from its massive head. The Ulun'suti, the jewel of power that lay embedded in the creature's skull, sparkled ominously in the bright sun.

Slowly, the Didanawisgi backed away from this horrific sight and began his descent down the mountain. He could not help but steal one more glance at the creature and marveled to himself, "How beautiful and terrible."

When Aganunitsi had reached level ground, he began to dig a massive, circular trench. The sun beat down angrily upon the hierophant, and biting flies and mosquitoes tormented him. Still, he finished his task and, after a short rest, began to gather pine cones. When he felt that he gathered a sufficient number, he placed them in the trench and set them ablaze. Thusly prepared, Aganunitsi warily made his way back up the mountain.

The Uktena was still soundly asleep, engrossed in dark dreams of violence and death. Aganunitsi closed his own eyes and sang a quiet song of prayer. Then, he aimed his arrow at the only weakness of the monster, the seventh band of color. With a loud twang, he let loose his arrow and ran down the mountainside, not even checking to see if the arrow had found its mark. He heard a loud hiss of pain and rage as the Uktena, though mortally wounded, tore through the underbrush hot on his trail. The medicine-man raced to his circular trench of burning pine cones and leapt over the roaring flames. He landed on his belly in the middle of the trench and ducked his head down while the Uktena spat its noxious poison in a blind rage. The corrosive poison melted trees and rocks and would have destroyed the hierophant as well, were it not for the flames of the trench. Instead, the mighty fires consumed the deadly poison, and the torrent of toxic blood that rained down from the Uktena's mortal wound was caught and contained by the trench. However, one drop of the Uktena's blood escaped the flames and landed on the medicine man's brow.

The Uktena

These creatures haunted the lakes and streams of the Southeast and preyed upon all living things that wandered too close to their watery lairs. The Uktena were old, perhaps as old as the making of the world itself, and their strength was colossal.

He never felt it. He was far too busy watching the massive titan crush tree and limb as it thrashed about in its final throes. After what seemed an eternity, the Uktena finally became caught in some tree trunks and stopped thrashing.

Aganunitsi was numb with disbelief. Had he done the impossible? Had he really killed the Uktena? He waited for some time before finally moving to action. He quickly realized that the powerful monster was just as fatal in death as it had been in life. The creature's blood was highly poisonous, and a deadly miasma had settled over the monster's carcass.

The holy man cleared his mind and stilled his thoughts while recalling an ancient song of power. With a mighty voice, he sang out to the birds of the land, and they came forth to his beck and call. The sky grew dark with their approach, and never before had so many birds descended in one place.

While under the approving eye of the Didanawisgi, the various avians began consuming the Uktena's body. For seven days, these birds feasted on the creature's decaying flesh until all that remained were the desiccated bones.

The hierophant then retrieved the powerful jewel from the scrapheap of bones and, true to his word, returned the Ulun'suti to the Cherokee. Aganunitsi reached an accord with those people, and between them there was peace at last. In time, he became a great healer and wonder-worker, accomplishing many feats hereto unheard of. His name became legend, and he lived out the long years of his life in peace. However, one thing perplexed the hierophant to the end of his days. When the single drop of blood from the Uktena's grievous wound had splashed upon Aganunitsi's brow, a small, green snake had grown from his forehead. Everyone could see the snake, except for the medicine-man himself. He never understood why people, upon first meeting him, gawked with such fear and trepidation. For many people, the little green serpent served as a constant reminder of the malevolent powers that glided in the darkness of the watery depths.

The Uktena was not the only creature of the waters to trouble the Cherokee. In some deep pools, such as those found in the French Broad, dwelt monstrous fish known as the Daktu. These aquatic terrors enjoyed overturning canoes and swallowing struggling fishermen whole.

The Tanaina of Alaska told tales of similar creatures said to have dwelt in the Iliamna Lake. These monsters were known as Big Fish, and they, too, troubled Early Man. With cunning patience, the Big Fish would wait until fishermen were far removed from the lake shores. These monsters would then bite holes in the boat hulls. This action forced the fishermen to leap into the frigid waters, where they were at the mercy of the Big Fish.

For the Lakota Sioux, the mysterious, murky depths were to be avoided at all cost, lest they stir up that which ought to rest forever in its black and foul abyss. The sinister creatures that the Lakota sought to avoid were known as the Unktehi.

THE AGE OF MYTHS & LEGENDS

Unlike many of the monsters mentioned earlier, the Unktehi were not merely creatures of instinct; they were calculated, cunning, and possessed sinister intent. These monsters were supernatural beings who commanded ghosts, owls, frogs, serpents, and lizards to carry out their evil bidding. They often took the form of great aquatic lizards or dragons and were covered with sea-green scales and horns. These creatures were the absolute rulers of their underwater realm, and they could cause damaging floods or devastating droughts according to their whims.

The old tales also say that the Unktehi made feasts of both Man and Beast when either ventured too close to lakes and streams. While the Lakota themselves could do little to harm these wicked creatures, there were benevolent spirits and supernatural beings that were willing to thwart the Unktehi's evil ways. Chief amongst these spirits of good were the Wakinyan, the Thunderbird. The Wakinyan took the form of gigantic eagles whose great flapping wings caused peels of thunder and from whose sharp eyes came forth lightning. The Unktehi fled to their deepest, darkest holes whenever Thunderbirds were abroad.

A similar scenario played itself out for the tribes of the Great Lakes as well. Unwholesome forces once dwelt in those waters, and they could change their shapes to suit their needs. These creatures were known as the Underwater Panthers, or Mishepishu. These beings were horned, scaled, and sometimes sported spikes or tufts of hair on their thorny backs. At other times, these monsters took on the forms of hideous panthers with great horns, massive eyes, and cold, copper scales.

It was believed that the Mishepishu lived in the deepest and darkest of lakes that dotted the northern landscape. From these haunts, these sinister beings were able to send bad weather to harry the dwellings of men. Like the dragons of Western Europe, Underwater Panthers also guarded immensely valuable treasure: copper. This metal was highly prized and useful to the tribes of the Great Lakes, but it was a perilous endeavor to steal copper from the Mishepishu. The sole purpose of this powerful creature was the pursuit of evil. However, the benign yet mighty Thunderbird, ever vigilant, held this creature's evil in check with a flash of lightning and a crash of thunder.

Even with their unwavering vigilance, the lords of thunder could not always detect the machinations of evil. Sometimes, the monsters of the deep were able to use guile and cunning to achieve their sinister deeds. In one tale told by the Passamaquoddy, the primal serpent, Kci-Athussos, used that most subtle and dangerous weapon of all to reach his ends. The weapon was love.

In an almost forgotten age, there was once a woman named Seskiku, who was so beautiful that she caught the attention of almost every man in the village. Her eyes were quiet pools of rich amber, and her hair was the color of blackest midnight. Her voice was as fair as a midsummer's breeze, and, when she smiled, it seemed that the whole world became a little bit brighter.

Daktu Hunt

In some deep pools, such as those found in the French Broad, dwelt monstrous fish known as the Daktu. These aquatic terrors enjoyed overturning canoes and swallowing struggling fishermen whole.

Glides In Darkness

The Unktehi were malignant supernatural beings who commanded ghosts, owls, frogs, serpents, and lizards to carry out their evil bidding. They often took the form of great aquatic lizards or dragons and were covered with sea-green scales and horns.

The Thunderbird

Chief amongst these spirits of good were the Wakinyan, the Thunderbird. The Wakinyan took the form of gigantic eagles whose great flapping wings caused peels of thunder and from whose sharp eyes came forth lightning.

It came as no surprise when the bravest and strongest warrior of the village asked Seskiku for her hand in marriage. She gladly accepted. What should have been a joyous occasion instead became a time of sorrow, as the young warrior died shortly after the marriage. Many were heartbroken for Seskiku, but more than a few young men were secretly pleased that she was available to their advances once more.

It was not long afterwards that another handsome suitor came to seek Seskiku's hand. As before, she accepted the handsome suitor's marriage request, and, once again, the village was abuzz with joyful celebration. Again tragedy struck, as the handsome suitor soon died a few days after the marriage ceremony. With the death of the second suitor, many in the village began to suspect that the young bride was cursed. Worried mothers forbade their sons to seek out Seskiku's hand in marriage, but, in the end, their efforts were to no avail. In the course of several months, three more suitors went to the beautiful young woman to ask for her hand in marriage. She accepted each marriage proposal, and all three suitors died in succession.

In the same village there lived a young man named Cikopu. Now it must be said that he was neither the bravest nor the most handsome warrior in the lands. However, he was certainly the cleverest. He, like many others in the village, suspected that Seskiku hid a strange and terrible secret. In time, Cikopu asked Seskiku for her hand in marriage, and she accepted. Many elders in the village shook their heads in pity for Cikopu, as they believed that he would soon be leaving the world of the living.

However, Cikopu possessed sharp eyes and a keen mind. When he wished, he could also travel unseen and unheard. He made good use of his abilities to watch and follow Seskiku throughout the month to discover her secret. Finally, the day of the marriage ceremony arrived, and Cikopu still had not learned why his predecessors had died. His guard was up, but, nonetheless, he still married Seskiku. Soon, they were off to a secluded spot in the forest to build a wigwam.

Seskiku designated the area in which to build the wigwam. She then left her husband so that she could gather nuts and berries. Cikopu, however, only pretended to construct the wigwam and instead silently followed his bride deeper into the forest. Seskiku continued for a time until she approached the stagnant shores of a small lake.

Cikopu felt a sense of foreboding as he quietly approached. Something was terribly wrong with this body of water, but Seskiku seemed oblivious. In fact, Seskiku had even undressed and stood at the water's edge. After gazing longingly at the lake for a few moments, she sang a song in a deep, guttural language that Cikopu could not understand. As Seskiku sang her strange song, the waters of the lake became troubled. Waves lapped the shoreline, and the young husband was suddenly seized with some nameless dread as he witnessed this strange tableau.

Out of the depths of the lake, a strange cry answered Seskiku's song. Cikopu watched in horror as a great crested serpent arose from the gray waters to regard the woman standing at the lake's edge. Cikopu knew what it was that lay before his wife, and he was afraid. In the old tales, this ancient evil was called Kci-Athussos. Despite Cikopu's concern for Seskiku, his first instinct was to race back to the village in terror. Such was the power of this crested serpent that it could incite fear and madness into the hearts of all but the bravest of beings.

Cikopu stayed hidden, transfixed with dread. As the serpent approached, Seskiku opened her arms wide to embrace the dark being. The serpent, in kind, gently wrapped its dark coils around the woman and sang a haunting song of power.

Cikopu did not know if the serpent had ensorcelled his wife with a love song or with illusion. Perhaps Seskiku believed that she embraced a handsome warrior instead of a cold, scaly monster born from the first age of creation, or mayhap she was a witch who had bargained with the ancient serpent for long life and power. In any event, Seskiku now belonged to Kci-Athussos, and Cikopu now understood what had happened to his predecessors. The serpent had placed his vile poison inside Seskiku. Seskiku, in turn, transferred the serpent's poison unto her husbands.

Slowly, Cikopu crept away from the foul lake. He was careful not to make even the slightest sound, lest he alert the terrible fiend to his presence. After what seemed an eternity, Cikopu finally made his way back to the encampment. Though his nerves were shaken, he decided to build the wigwam that his ensorcelled wife had asked for. In the span of a few hours, he finished his task, and, just as he was about to build a fire, Seskiku returned.

Seskiku approached Cikopu with knowing eyes and made to embrace him. Cikopu quickly turned from her and made himself busy by gathering cordage. Puzzled, Seskiku silently watched him as he constructed two beds. Eventually, the shadows lengthened, and a sickle moon rose in the distance. Cikopu then retired to his bed, watching his wife all the while.

Seskiku then made to lay with him, but her husband sternly reproached her by saying, "Tonight we sleep separately. If you get lonely, you can go sleep with your friend in the waters."

Seskiku's eyes widened in surprise, and a sharp gasp escaped her lips. Somehow, he had discovered her secret. Her eyes darted about the wigwam for something to harm her husband with, but Cikopu was too clever. He had hidden his bow outside the wigwam, and he kept his hunting knife close by his side. With an air of defeat, Seskiku lay in her bed and went to sleep. Cikopu watched her throughout the night and was prepared to defend himself if needed. However, his wife never stirred.

After a long night, morning finally came. Tired and groggy, Cikopu tried to wake his sleeping wife, but there was no response. He rose and gently shook her shoulder to wake her. To his surprise, he found that she was dead. The poison of the ancient serpent had stilled her heart. Though Cikopu mourned his loss, he reminded himself that the poison that had killed his wife was meant for him. Slowly he returned to the village to tell the tribal council of all that had transpired. It was then decided that Seskiku's body would not be cared for in the way of the Passamaquoddy. Instead, Cikopu and a retinue of the bravest warriors returned her body to the lake of Kci-Athussos. Her husband placed Seskiku on the gray, placid waters, and her body gently floated to the center of the lake. Without warning, a great serpent's tail wrapped its coils around Seskiku and took her body into the dark, cold abyss.

Primordial Serpent

In the old tales, this ancient evil was called Kci-Athussos. Despite Cikopu's concern for Seskiku, his first instinct was to race back to the village in terror. Such was the power of this crested serpent that it could incite fear and madness into the hearts of all but the bravest of beings.

Not all of the terrors of the deep were reptilian or serpentine in form and nature. From the Great Plains to the Rocky Mountains came many strange tales of a mysterious people who spent their solitary days bathing in the rivers and streams. In some tales, they appeared to be diminutive men and women with long shiny hair and skin the color of bronze. In other stories, they could appear as small, horrific monsters who terrorized stray hunters and fishermen who had stumbled upon their watery haunts.

These dark beings were known as Water Babies. To even see one of these creatures was an omen of ill portent, for it meant that a loved one would soon die. Malicious creatures, Water Babies enjoyed playing mean-spirited pranks upon the unwary. At times, they would lead hunters astray during the night with foxfire. On other occasions, they stole unsupervised children and babies. However, it was their chief delight and hobby to drown the unsuspecting bathers and swimmers that had trespassed into their pools. With speed and strength that belied their size, the Water Babies would latch onto their helpless victims and drag them down into their cold, sunless realms, never to be seen again.

The Merced River of the Yosemite Valley was a place of fear and dread, not only because it lay in the territory of a man-eating giant, but also because of cruel beings called the Hohape. These mermaid-like creatures guarded their river jealously and wouldn't hesitate to drown the Southern Miwok who trespassed too near their waters. However, brave mortals could sometimes trade man-made objects with the Hohape for the precious shells and pearls that lay in their watery realm.

In the old days, both the Paiute and Miwok feared waterfalls, rapids, or any other area where the waters were restless and disturbed. It was believed by these tribal peoples that the Nunu, powerful destructive spirits of nature, dwelt in these places. The Nunu would violently consume any man, woman, or child that ventured too close to their borders.

For the Southern Cheyenne, an underwater monster to be wary of was the Mihn. The few people that had seen this menacing creature and lived to tell of the encounter described the monster as a great lizard with horns on its head and a scaly body partially covered with gray hair. Large bodies of water, like the Missouri River, were once thought to house these creatures. Travelers across such waterways were always in danger of the Mihn overturning the boats and swallowing the passengers whole. The Thunderbird, ever the enemy of evil, sometimes struck the waters with his mighty thunderbolts. The crash of lightning always sent the Mihn scurrying away.

In the frozen North, the Central Inuit were eternally on guard against the evil Amikuk, a terrible sea monster that could change its shape into that of a seal. In this form, the Amikuk lured hunters far away from land and into the icy seas. Far from help, the hunters would realize too late that they had been deceived by the Amikuk's clever ruse. More often than not, the hunters would be dragged from their kayaks and into the frozen depths, never to be seen or heard from again.

In Seneca lore, the bane of all existence was the shape-shifting being known as Doonongaes, which means "He-of-the-Two-Horns." As its name implies, this creature took on a serpentine aspect, with two curved horns jutting from its massive head. This diabolical creature reveled in wanton destruction. He was also the source of all sickness and diseases that had plagued the tribes of the north. Doonongaes was even able to infuse a portion of his evil will into his surroundings. His watery abode was so infected with his potent magic that mortals who touched the waters would die in agony. In his dark watery realm, Doonongaes was not alone. He was protected by a giant turtle named Skahnowa. He, too, enjoyed spreading pain and misery. These two wicked creatures were ever at war with the mighty spirit, Hinon the Thunderer. Were it not for the unrelenting efforts of Hinon, the wicked intent of Doonongaes and Skahnowa might have consumed the world.

The Creek, Seminole, Yuchi and Choctaw of Southeastern Oklahoma once avoided certain springs and lakes, because they believed that the ever watchful Tie Snake lay in wait. Descriptions of these serpents varied. Some tales held that Tie Snakes were gigantic serpents of green hue. Other tales said that Tie Snakes were pitch black and not much larger than a normal snake. However, their strength was such that they could pull a horsed rider from his mount at full gallop.

Some tales even said that Tie Snakes were sentient and could speak with Man when it suited the serpents' needs. To converse with a Tie Snake was a very dangerous thing, though. These ancient serpents were exceedingly clever, and they could trick the unwary into bad endings. Only once have the intelligent Tie Snakes been outwitted. That particular feat was accomplished by Master Rabbit, the eternal trickster.

With that said, there are some tales that speak of the Tie Snakes' kindness to lost children. In those tales, the Lord of the Tie Snakes always sent such children home laden with many gifts. In other tales, Tie Snakes were said to spirit children away to their underwater lairs, where these children would remain captive forever.

Most tales agreed that these underwater serpents bore one or two multicolored horns upon their heads. Like the Uktena's flashing jewel, the horn of the Tie Snake was an item of great power coveted by holy men. With a piece of the Tie Snake's horn, a medicine-man might heal the sick, drive away evil spirits, or become well-nigh impervious to knife, spear, axe or arrow. A mortal who possessed a Tie Snake's horn could even exercise his will over the other creatures of the lakes and streams. Fish could be made to fill the fisherman's nets. Otters and beavers could be compelled to surrender their lives for their valuable furs. Even water fowl could be made to stand still so that the hunter's arrow would find its mark. These miracles were so enticing that some holy men hatched elaborate plans to subdue the Tie Snakes for their powerful horns. However, only the most powerful or foolish of hierophants would even dare to kill or capture these powerful serpents.

Below

Malicious creatures, Water Babies enjoyed playing mean-spirited pranks upon the unwary. At times, they would lead hunters astray during the night with foxfire. On other occasions, they stole unsupervised children and babies. However, it was their chief delight and hobby to drown the unsuspecting bathers and swimmers that had trespassed into their pools.

Guardian

These mermaid-like creatures guarded their river jealously and wouldn't hesitate to drown the Southern Miwok who trespassed too near their waters. However, brave mortals could sometimes trade man-made objects with the Hohape for the precious shells and pearls that lay in their watery realm.

He Of The Two Horns

In Seneca lore, the bane of all existence was the shape-shifting being known as Doonongaes, which means "He-of-the-Two-Horns." As its name implies, this creature took on a serpentine aspect, with two curved horns jutting from its massive head. This diabolical creature reveled in wanton destruction.

Lying In Wait

Some tales held that Tie Snakes were gigantic serpents of green hue. Other tales said that Tie Snakes were pitch black and not much larger than a normal snake. However, their strength was such that they could pull a horsed rider from his mount at full gallop.

Apparently, though, some of the Wise must have been successful. There are some legends that speak of heroes and holy men who carried pieces of the coveted horn with them. However, many of the old tales concerning Tie Snakes usually ended in tragedy for those mortals who had sought to contend with the malignant creatures of the cold, murky depths.

Chapter Three

Masters of Wood and Water

CHAPTER THREE

Masters of Wood and Water

"For know by lot from Jove I am the power
Of this fair wood and live in oaken bower,
To nurse the saplings tall, and curl the grove
With ringlets quaint and wanton windings wove;
And all my plants I save from nightly ill
Of noisome winds and Blasting vapors chill;"
-Arcades - John Milton

    According to the old tales, a race of mysterious yet powerful spirits once haunted the windswept plains, lonely forest, and snow-enshrouded peaks. These beings were akin to the mighty race of giants in that they, too, were living, breathing embodiments of the Earth's power. Whereas the giants came to embody all that was chaotic and destructive in Nature's mosaic, these little beings came to represent the constructive purpose and order of the very Earth itself.

    The Little People, as their name implies, were diminutive beings who varied in height from six inches to three feet. Many tales describe them as being perfectly formed men and women with long, silky black hair and possessed of a cold, unearthly beauty. Like their giant brethren, these beings were old, old enough to remember the birth of the Earth itself.

    Because of this intimacy with the world, all of the Earth's secrets were laid bare to them. They knew the tongues of all living things, whether they be bird, beast, tree, or man. They were also great wonder-workers, able to cast enchanting illusion or horrifying nightmares. They were able to walk unclad and unseen to mortal eyes or they were able to change their shape and form into that of an animal. Their potent songs of power and enchantment were without equal, differing greatly from the songs of the Wise. The hierophant, through years of discipline, learned to attune him or herself to Nature and was thus able to hear and mimic the distant song of the Earth. In essence, the medicine-person derived his or her strength and power from the natural world. In comparison, the power of the little people was rooted in the essence of their very beings, rather than extracted from the Earth. Besides, if mortal men could vaguely hear the Earth's distant chant, the Little People could, without a medium, speak directly to the Earth itself. For this reason, North American tribes honored and respected the little people. At times, tribal members made offerings and effigies to placate these mighty beings.

    The Little People were known by many names across the vast North American continent. To the Quinault, they were known as Stick Indians. The overall character of these Stick Indians could be described as ambiguous at best. While not particularly evil, these Little People did enjoy playing mean-spirited pranks on solitary hunters. Sometimes these Little People could be so bothersome that it became common practice for hunters and fishermen to leave shiny objects while in their domain. These Little People were mesmerized, and, conveniently, distracted by sparkling objects.

To the Kickapoo, the Little People served as protectors to sacred places. They were also enforcers of cultural taboos and morals. These powerful beings were called the Muchee-Muna-Toe, and so respected were these Little People that it was taboo even to speak of them, except during the winter months.

The Comanche knew the Little People by the name, Nuna-Pee. It was said that, on certain moonlit nights, the drums of these Little People could be heard echoing in the distant hills. However, it was perilous to seek the Nuna-Pee out, because they possessed invisible arrows capable of killing any mortal who trespassed too near their abode.

The Northern Ute named their Little People Mookich. These shy spirits lived in cliff dwellings well off the beaten path. Hunters were wise to leave offerings of tobacco, coins, small pieces of rope, or food whenever traveling through the Mookich domain. To do so ensured that these Little People would not be so inclined to harass the hunters or cause mischief around the camp.

Ponca and Omaha tales speak of the Gada'zhe and Ni'Kashinga Man'tanaha, the "wild ones." These dangerous Little People were able to injure mortals internally without even piercing the flesh or spilling blood. They also had the disturbing habit of kidnapping young children.

Among the tribes of the Iroquois Confederacy existed tales of the mighty Jogah. These Little People were the protective spirits of nature who kept the natural order of the world in total balance. Without them, it was believed that all life on the Earth would die. These nature spirits were divided into three groups: the Gandayak, the Ohdowas, and the Gahongas. The Gandayak held all forest and rivers under their protection. The Ohdowas lived underground and held almost all poisonous creatures and monsters in check, while the Gahongas warded the mountains and hills.

The Canotila, or "tree dwellers," were a solitary Little People who were both feared and honored by both the Lakota and Dakota peoples. These powerful beings served as messengers between the world of the living and the world of spirits. However, some of the Canotila enjoyed causing sickness and injury to humans, usually solitary hunters or fishermen. The Sioux dreaded to even see these creatures, for doing so meant that a close relative would soon die.

The Creek Nation called the Little People I'sti Lupu'ski. Often times, tribal members had to employ the services of powerful medicine-men to counteract these Little People's dangerous magic. Adept shapeshifters, it was not unheard of for hunters to be led astray deep into the dim forest by the wily I'sti Lupu'ski. On a darker note, they were also known to cause madness in even the hale and strong.

The Miwok feared the volatile nature spirit, Nenakatu, who not only had power over the waters but also possessed the ability to mesmerize her victims. This powerful being sometimes wore the appearance of a small, wizened woman with long, black hair that swept the ground. Like the Canotila of Sioux lore, to even see the Nenakatu was an omen of ill portent.

The Catawba people of South Carolina avoided certain vales and deep forests, because they were the known haunts of the Yehasu'rie, the "wild people." These mysterious Little People lived deep underground and subsisted on turtles, roots, tadpoles, and acorns. Private beings, the wild people shunned mortals, unless they were on raids to steal items such as knives, whetstones, jewelry, or feathers from tribal campgrounds. However, should a man or woman accidentally stumble into their domain, only then would the Yehasu'rie make their presence abundantly known. Out of spite, these creatures would tangle a horse's hair, kidnap children, and frighten hunters with their disconcerting child-like cries. They also possessed magically charged arrows that could maim or kill their intended victims without the victim even realizing the damage until it was too late.

Little Hunters

To the Quinault, they were known as Stick Indians. Sometimes these Little People could be so bothersome that it became common practice for hunters and fishermen to leave shiny objects while in their domain. The Little People were fascinated, mesmerized, and, conveniently, distracted by sparkling objects.

Nuna-Pee All Around

The Comanche knew the Little People by the name, Nuna-Pee. It was said that, on certain moonlit nights, the drums of these Little People could be heard echoing in the distant hills. However, it was perilous to seek the Nuna-Pee out, because they possessed invisible arrows capable of killing any mortal who trespassed too near their abode.

It is important to note that not all groups of Little People were so perilous to mankind. Some groups were simply watchful and uneasy when in the company of mortals. One such group was the May-may-gway-shi of Algonquin folklore. These small, hairy beings were believed to have carved the ancient petroglyphs among the caves and cliffs of the North. The May-may-gway-shi were also known for their love of fish. In that long ago age, it was not so uncommon to see small canals dug along the river banks that teemed with life. These canals were supposedly the workings of the May-may-gway-shi which they used to stock with their favorite fish. At other times, when they were in need and bold enough, the Little People would make stealthy incursions into tribal camps to steal from the fishermen's nets. Easily frightened, the May-may-gway-shi could travel at tremendous speeds, either on foot or in their small stone canoes. Upon entering a stony outcrop or cliff, they would enter the rock face and vanish. It has been said that certain holy men, wise in the lore of the land, could sometimes enter the May-may-gway-shi's stony abode and trade tobacco for the powerful Earth medicine of these Little People.

Some Little People were even considered allies of Man and could be counted on to assist certain tribes in their times of need. Tales exist among the Alabama-Coushatta of the benevolent, yet enigmatic, Atosee and how a hunter gained their everlasting friendship.

Once, in the days of the grandfathers, a mighty hunter of the Coushatta decided to travel to a village in the distant west. He packed all of the essential tools that he thought he would use and then set off on his chosen path. The first few days of his journey were uneventful. The mighty hunter traveled far during the daylight hours and, at night, built a lean-to to sleep in. He hunted or fished when his rations grew short. The deeper he trekked into the forest, the more he felt a sense of unease.

His sharp senses told him that he was not alone in these wild lands, far from the dwellings of men. As the days progressed, he imagined that he could hear the voices of many people trailing him from a distance. Despite his best efforts to discover his pursuers, he never saw another soul in the forest.

In time, he began to suspect that he was being followed by the Atosee. He had heard many tales concerning these Little People, and not all of the stories were good. The Atosee were powerful beings, and they were known to be capricious at best. The hunter had also heard that the Atosee were very shy around mortals and rarely made their presence known. He did not know why these beings were following him, but, in a strange way, he began to find their hidden presence a comfort. The journey was long, and the hunter was lonely. Perhaps that is why he placed a piece of bear fat for the Little People outside of his camp one night.

The next morning, he awoke with a start as a band of the Little People peered at him from behind the trees and bushes. These mystical beings were no more than a few inches tall, and many wore sea shells as armor, while their hair was adorned with hummingbird feathers. One of the Atosee, who was clearly the leader of this band, stepped forward and spoke to the hunter in a strange language that almost sounded like the chirping of birds. To the hunter's surprise, he could understand every word that the Little Person spoke.

He learned that this band was, in fact, a war party and that they were also heading to the far west. The hunter was fascinated by the thought of the Atosee going to war. He asked them many questions. Who or what were their enemies? Were they monsters? Or were they another tribe of Little People? In the end, the Atosee said very little concerning their upcoming battle.

Instead, the Little People were far more concerned with food and asked the hunter if he had any rations. He did not, so they decided to go hunting together. The hunter and the Atosee wandered deeper into the forest and soon came upon a hare.

In one swift motion, the Coushatta hunter nocked his arrow and felled the rabbit with one well-placed shot. The Little People shouted with glee and raced to collect the hare. The Atosee wished to skin and field-dress the rabbit on the spot, but the hunter took the rabbit back to the camp. Once at the campsite, the hunter carefully prepared the rabbit and offered it to the Little People, but they ate very little. The hunter ate the greater portion. Fully sated, the man went to sleep while the Little People kept watch throughout the night.

At first sunrise, the party broke camp and journeyed westward. While they traveled, the Little People regaled the hunter with wonderful tales of brave heroes, horrid monsters, and strange, wondrous lands. The party traveled far, and, as the descending sun set the evening sky ablaze with hues of yellow and red, the band encountered a large, black bear. The Little People gave chase and urged the hunter to help them hunt the bear, but the hunter was hesitant. He doubted that he could kill such a large animal with his arrows. He was utterly astonished when the Little People felled the beast with their diminutive arrows and darts. Truly, the Atosee were mighty. The hunter wished to field-dress the bear on the spot, but, to his surprise, the Little People grabbed the bear and took it back to camp. Once the party arrived at the camp, they prepared and cooked the bear over the open fire. The hunter ate very little, while the Atosee ate the greatest portion.

On the following day of travel, the troupe encountered a small brook. The hunter leapt from one embankment to the other and patiently waited for the Little People to follow suit. He was puzzled when they stood on the other side of the stream in distress. It appeared that the Atosee could not cross the running water. The hunter found a thick log and placed it across the stream. The Little People raced across to the other side.

Farther down their path, they approached a raging river. The hunter was dismayed when he realized that he could not cross this violent body of water. The Atosee merely smiled and gathered several logs. With their small cunning hands, they created a stable raft which the hunter was able to use to cross the river. The band then set up camp and rested for the night.

The next day, the hunter noticed that the Little People were far more reticent and rarely spoke, even to each other. At midday, the Atosee began to sing songs of war, and they painted their bodies red for battle. The hunter was both mystified and anxious by their activity. The leader of the Atosee finally spoke to the hunter and explained that they were drawing near to their enemy and that this would be a hard-pitched battle. Some of the Atosee would not return home. The hunter grew truly frightened, but he was determined to help the Little People in any way that he could. Once the little people were girded for the war, they marched on to the west. As they traveled, the hunter heard a low, droning sound that only grew louder and louder as they went.

Suddenly, the leader of the Atosee halted, and the hunter looked ahead in anticipation of danger. At first, the hunter saw nothing- certainly no giants or man-eating serpents. Instead, the hunter saw a large hive of yellow-jacket wasps. Granted, it was surely the largest hive the hunter had ever seen, but his fear immediately left him, and he almost laughed at the seriousness of the Atosee. However, the leader of Atosee assured him that these wasps were magical creatures and truly were dangerous to all living things. The hunter then noticed that, as the wasp flew to and fro about their hive, a strange, shimmering light began to emanate from their golden bodies.

With a loud cry of defiance, the Little People raced to the hive and started firing arrows and darts at their airborne foes. The battle was like nothing the hunter had ever seen. The Atosee's movements were almost too fast to follow, and many wasps fell in the initial onslaught. The winged insects recovered quickly, though, and they attacked the Little People with equal ferocity.

Mischief Maker

The Creek Nation called the Little People I'sti Lupu'ski. Adept shape-shifters, it was not unheard of for hunters to be led astray deep into the dim forest by the wily I'sti Lupu'ski. On a darker note, they were also known to cause madness in even the hale and strong.

A Dangerous Being

The Miwok feared the volatile nature spirit, Nenakatu, who not only had power over the waters but also possessed the ability to mesmerize her victims. This powerful being sometimes wore the appearance of a small, wizened woman with long, black hair that swept the ground. Like the Canotila of Sioux lore, to even see the Nenakatu was an omen of ill portent.

Unseen Marksman

The Catawba people of South Carolina avoided certain vales and deep forests because they were the known haunts of the Yehasu'rie, the "wild people." They possessed magically charged arrows that could maim or kill their intended victims without the victim even realizing the damage until it was too late.

May-may-gway-shi

Easily frightened, the May-may-gway-shi could travel at tremendous speeds, either on foot or in their small stone canoes. Upon entering a stony outcrop or cliff, they would enter the rock face and vanish.

To the hunter's shock, some of the Little People fell in combat, as several wasps latched on to the Atosee and stung them to death. Still, the battle raged on, and both sides seemed evenly matched. In time, the battle turned against the Atosee. It seemed that, whenever a magical wasp fell, it was quickly replaced by two more equally vicious combatants.

The hunter watched in dread, as there were now only a handful of the Atosee left to battle against the unrelenting army of wasps. The hunter had seen enough. He raced away from the battle and found a large, dry bush. He quickly built a fire and set the dry bush ablaze. With his flaming brand, he raced back to the battle and batted away the magical wasps that tried to attack him. The flame and smoke dismayed the insects, and most left the field of battle. The hunter then climbed the tree of the wasps and struck their hive repeatedly with the flaming brand until it was nothing more than burnt, tattered refuse.

The Little People were very grateful to the hunter for his contributions in battle, so they presented him with many gifts and blessings. From that day forth, there was a great friendship between the Atosee and the Alabama-Coushatta. It was a friendship that would last until the end of days.

For the Choctaw, the powerful little person known as the Kawnakuasha was a mysterious being that aided medicine-men in their search for healing herbs and curative items. It was said that this little person was sometimes directly responsible for introducing medicine-men into the powerful profession of healing in the first place.

Sometimes, lost or runaway children had the good fortune to be found and rescued by the Kawnakuasha. Before returning a child home, the kindly little person first took them to his distant lands. Once they had arrived at the Kawnakuasha's cave, they were greeted by three ancient spirits of the Earth who appeared as small, old women.

To the child, they brought three items: a sharp knife, a bowl of poisonous plants, and a bowl of curative herbs. If the child chose to take the knife, he would grow to be a craven, dishonorable man prone to violent outburst. If the child chose the bowl of poisonous plants, he would grow up unable to distinguish good from bad, proving to be an unreliable individual at best. If the child chose the third bowl of healing herbs, he was destined to become a great healer and prominent figure in his tribe.

The Kawnakuasha and the three little women would then confer upon the child all the knowledge and lore needed to become a wonder-worker. For three days, the child would stay with these Little People, after which time he was returned home safe and sound. However, the child would be forbidden to talk about where he had been and what he had seen. Only when the child had reached adulthood would he be permitted to use his vast healing knowledge for the betterment of his people.

To the Cherokee, the kind-spirited Little People of the mountains and forest were known as the Yunwi Tsundi. They were perfectly shaped and beautiful, often times dressed entirely in white. These helpful sprites guided lost hunters home and, like the Kawnakuasha, helped medicine-men find healing herbs.

A gentle race, they rejoiced in the presence of children. At times, they would bring young ones to their mystical dwellings deep within the mountains before returning the children home laden with gifts. It was also said that the Little People would approach tribal dwellings in the night to partake in daily chores. However, to watch them work could be dangerous; seeing them could mean that a loved one may soon die.

As kind and generous as the Yunwi Tsundi were, they still were a secretive, mysterious folk. These Little People dealt with intruding adults by casting a pall of enchantment upon them. They also did not abide thieves of any sort. Should a mortal discover an object such as a knife, trinket, or ribbon deep within the forest, it was prudent to just leave the item be. If the object was too tempting not to retrieve, it was then wise to leave an offering of tobacco and to ask for permission to take the item first. The valuable object in question could very well belong to the Little People. To take items without asking for permission would enrage the Yunwi Tsundi, and they would mercilessly pelt the transgressor with sharp rocks.

Like the Jogah of Iroquois tales, the Yunwi Tsundi were divided into three branches: the Dogwood People, the Laurel People, and the Rock People. Of the three, the Dogwood People were the kindest and aided people in many ways, sometimes giving advice through dreams. The Laurel People were the mischievous pranksters apt to hide important items or weapons. When children laughed in their sleep, it was supposedly the work of the Laurel People sharing their favorite jokes with the sleeping young ones. The Rock People were ill-tempered and jealously guarded their territory. These mean-spirited sprites stole babies and shot invisible arrows at people, which accounted for the sharp pains some older adults felt in the morning. However, it was not the Yunwi Tsundi's abilities that made them so well remembered; rather, it was their kindness.

Hundreds of years before they were driven away from their homeland by European and American conquests, the Cherokee dwelt near the mighty and mysterious Smoky Mountains. Life, though difficult, was good for these people, and almost all of the Cherokee had plenty of food and shelter, so long as everyone in the village did his or her part and remained constructive. So, it was not surprising when one Cherokee father grew increasingly distraught by the actions of his frolicsome son.

While most boys were busy learning the skills they would need to survive as men in this harsh age, this father's son was busy wiling away the days in play and song. The boy partook in so much play and song that the people began to call his son, "Forever Boy." Forever Boy would shirk all responsibility and run through the green meadows or pass the days lazily floating down the gently flowing streams.

In frustration, the boy's father confronted his son and made this ultimatum: "My son, it is unbecoming for a boy of your age to relinquish all responsibility. You cannot spend the rest of your days in play. Therefore, in two days' time, I shall send you to your uncle. He will teach you all the things you need to know to become a man." "But father!" cried Forever Boy, "that is too cruel. I do not wish to grow up! Please spare me this cruel punishment!" "Son," answered the father in a sad voice, "this is not a punishment. All living things must grow older. Look at the stalk of corn or the mighty tree. These things, too, were young and tender at one time, but they grew. The animals of the forest and fields must also grow older. It is a law of nature that cannot be disobeyed. It is only the Nunnehi and the Yunwi Tsundi that do not abide by this law and grow older. We are not Nunnehi. We are not Yunwi Tsundi. We are men, and we must grow older."

Gathering Herbs

For the Choctaw, the powerful little person known as the Kawnakuasha was a mysterious being that aided medicine-men in their search for healing herbs and curative items. It was said that this little person was sometimes directly responsible for introducing medicine-men into the powerful profession of healing in the first place.

Forever Boy, weeping profusely, raced away from his father's home and ran deep into the woods. He slowly made his way to a river and sobbed, "This is unfair. Must I give up all the wonderful games and enchanted places of the wild?"

In utter sadness, Forever Boy sat by the riverbank and sang a song. His voice was beautiful, and, for a moment, it seemed as though the entire forest grew silent to hear his lament. When he finished singing, he laid on his back to watch the trees sway back and forth in the gentle breeze for what he thought would be the last time. Suddenly, his solace was interrupted by the sound of pleasant laughter. He sprang to his feet but saw no one there. "Forever Boy," called a playful voice. "Why do you weep?" Forever Boy called out defiantly, "Who's there? How do you know me?" Again, laughter cascaded from the trees above and from the bushes that grew near the river's edge. "We know you, Forever Boy. We have seen you at play among the cypress and willow. We have seen you run and frolic with the animals of the forest and fields. Will you now play with us, Forever Boy? We are the Yunwi Tsundi, the Little People."

Appearing from the shadows of the trees stepped forth a small man, no taller than an infant. His skin was golden, and his hair was long and black. He wore a white shirt that seemed to shimmer like the sunlight upon the water. Other similar beings stepped forth into the light. Some were male, others female, but all were stunningly beautiful. All fear left Forever Boy's heart, and he gladly accepted the Yunwi Tsundi's invitation.

He taught the Little People his favorite games, and they, in turn, taught him the names of all the plants and animals of the forest. They laughed, sang, and played all day, until the sky turned red and the sun sank beyond the western horizon. Forever Boy wept when he saw the first stars of the evening sky twinkle into being. "I must leave you, my friends. Soon I will be forced to go to my uncle to become a man. I will not be able to play with you ever again, but I will always remember you." The Little People were stricken with sadness. Never before had they met such an enjoyable young child. Therefore, the Yunwi Tsundi held a council amongst themselves. Though Forever Boy listened and watched intently, he could not understand the Little People, because they spoke in their own light and flitting tongue. When they finished deliberating, they turned to Forever Boy.

"Forever Boy, given the choice, which would you chose? To return home with our blessing, growing to become a mighty warrior and great man of your people? Or to remain a boy forever and stay with us?"

Forever Boy leapt with joy. He decided to remain a boy forever and to spend his days singing and laughing with his new friends for all time. The Yunwi Tsundi were overjoyed and immediately leapt into song and dance. They filled the evening air with their laughter. Later that night, a messenger of the Yunwi Tsundi made his way to the father of Forever Boy. He explained that the boy had chosen to remain with the Little People and would be well cared for. Though the boy's father was saddened by the loss of his son, he was also thankful that the little people had bestowed upon his son the greatest gift imaginable: eternal youth.

All in all, the Little People were not truly wicked creatures like the other supernatural beings of that age. Rather, as beings born in the First Age of Creation, they simply had altogether different ideas and values. These were older, wilder ideas and values that centered upon the overall well-being and balance of the natural world. Over the centuries, as Man retreated from Nature and into himself, was it any wonder that the general attitude displayed by the Little People concerning selfish mortals ranged from wary tolerance to unrelenting hostility?

Chapter Four

Denizens of the Dark

CHAPTER FOUR

Denizens of the Dark

"Like one who, on a lonely road,
Doth walk in fear and dread,
And, having once turned round, walks on,
And turns no more his head;
Because he knows a frightful fiend
Doth close behind him tread."
-Rime of the Ancient Mariner- Samuel Taylor Coleridge

For the Ojibwa, the winters of the north could be long and harsh ordeals. Snowstorms could suddenly spring up to obscure the once familiar landscape with blinding, white cruelty. Bitter, howling winds could pierce the warmest of furs to freeze a man's heart and soul.

While hypothermia and starvation were the chief concerns for the hunters of old, a darker and much more sinister danger was once thought to have stalked the gray, frozen shores and ice-enshrouded landscape. This malevolent force had many names but was most commonly known by the tribes of the region as the Wintiko or Wendigo.

It was a gigantic creature of enormous strength and size, composed entirely of ice. However, some of the old tales say that inside the creature's ice-enshrouded body was a normal, human body that wore the frozen corpus as a shell. These wicked creatures stalked hunters in the night and regularly made meals of anyone unfortunate enough to meet them, hence their moniker, the "cannibal giants." Yet, it was not their deeds, though terrible, that made these creatures so widely feared. It was a horrifying fact that anyone could become a Wendigo. Just seeing a Wendigo could cause a person to transform into one of these cold-hearted beasts.

Committing the horrible act of cannibalism would also result in the loss of humanity. A transformation into one of these supernatural beasts was sure to follow. Even dreaming of the Wendigo could cause a person to become one of these monsters. However, there are some old tales that speak of men who were able to transform into a Wendigo at will. One such tale concerns the great Ojibwa hunter, Makobimide, and how he and his four brave wives encountered the supernatural.

Once, in the days of yore, the mighty hunter, Makobimide, returned home from a long day of hunting deeply troubled. Though he wore a grim expression on his face, he said very little to his four wives. A great bear of a man, he sat down heavily on his bench. He quietly ate the meal of nine rabbits that his wives had prepared for him. Then he rose and stood by the fire, deep in thought. After some time, he mumbled quietly, "I met a strange man in the woods today. He is coming over to see me tonight. I will wait for him."

The four wives grew terribly afraid, because they understood Makobimide's somber mood and somewhat cryptic statement. The four wives knew that the forthcoming visitor was an evil sorcerer who had gained the power to become a Wendigo at will. Makobimide instructed his wives to melt tallow in a large kettle and to keep the contents piping hot. As the sun hung low on the western horizon, the husband and wives heard the evil sorcerer call from outside. Makobimide hugged his wives goodbye and then stepped out to meet his fate.

When the sorcerer saw the hunter approach, he smiled with malevolent glee. He then screamed into the chill evening air eight times. Each time that a scream issued from his lips, he became larger and larger until, at last, he stood taller than a pine. His limbs were twisted at odd angles, and his body was completely covered by a thick sheet of ice. His lips were peeled back, revealing black gums and decaying teeth.

The hunter, Makobimide, breathed in the frigid air and then screamed forth his challenge as well. Ten times he screamed, and each time he grew taller and taller, even greater in height and stature than the wicked creature that stood before him. He, too, had become a Wendigo. The ground groaned as the two gigantic adversaries faced each other.

With their powerful arms, each combatant savagely ripped up trees by their roots and used them as crude clubs. The ensuing battle between the two Wendigo was terrible yet magnificent. Like the Titans of old, these two creatures filled the evening air with screams of rage and bellows of agony as they struggled to overcome each other. The mountains and valleys echoed with their battle. The waters of the Great Lakes were also troubled and violently crashed upon the shores, reflecting the unbridled fury of the two supernatural adversaries.

The sun sank below the western horizon, and the first stars of night twinkled into being, yet the two Wendigo fought on, oblivious to the world around them.

At last, Makobimide struck the evil Wendigo with such force that the creature's head shattered into a hundred pieces. Though Makobimide was a Wendigo himself, he still retained enough of his human sensibilities to build a massive fire with which to melt the evil Wendigo's body.

When this deed was done, the transformed hunter made his way home. He ignored the growing urge to stalk off into the night in search of human prey. Faithfully waiting at the door of his house stood his four wives with the boiling kettle of tallow.

He gently bent down to the doorway of his dwelling and opened his mouth. The four wives then poured the boiling contents of the kettle into his large gaping maw. Immediately, the hunter began to shrink back to his regular size, and the ice began to melt off of his body.

Makobimide and his wives had not only survived an encounter with the malevolent but had even managed to banish this evil creature from the world of men for all time.

Makobimide was able to destroy a Wendigo with brute force by shattering its head. This was one of the few ways in which these creatures could be slain. The only other way to destroy a Wendigo was to melt the monster's heart of ice, a daunting task in itself. Yet there exists an intriguing old tale that not only includes an unusual Wendigo as the antagonist but also involves the magical race of little people as well.

Long ago, a young couple married and were soon blessed with a beautiful child. The early months were happy times for the young family, until the mother began to notice her baby's strange behavior. There were times when her newborn would stare at her with sharp, calculating eyes while listening intently to all she said. It was almost as if he could understand her. The couple's infant almost never laughed, and he rarely smiled. When the baby did smile, adults could not help but feel uncomfortable. The baby exuded an aura of vile cunning and intelligence. In time, a nameless dread had begun to gnaw at the young mother's heart, but she simply dismissed these emotions with an apprehensive chuckle and carried out her daily chores.

Not far away, on the shores of a small lake, lived a powerful spirit named Manidogizik. This mighty manido had devoted his life to the service of good. He often visited families in their times of need. The young mother decided to enlist the manido's services. If anyone could treat her child, it was Manidogizik. Before seeking his help, the young mother met with an older woman from the village to discuss the manido's payment, as well as the proper protocol when dealing with the wise spirit. All the while, the infant listened with great interest, until the older woman said her goodbyes and left. A cold smile crept on the baby's face, and, in a voice barely above a whisper, the infant chuckled, "Where does this supposedly all-powerful manido live? Someday I'm going to go and visit him."

The young mother stared at her baby in dread. It was unheard of for a child to speak at such an early age. In a wavering voice, she shakily replied, "You...you should not speak that way about Manidogizik."

She picked up her child and placed him in his cradle-board. In vain, she tried to forget her child's chilling words and focused on her daily chores. She wrestled with the impulse to race out of her home to tell someone-anyone-about her baby's startling ability to speak. In the end, she decided it would be prudent to keep her baby's ability a secret. After all, who would believe her?

On most nights, the young parents would place the baby in his cradle-board between them when they slept. One night, the young mother awoke to find her baby missing. Seized with a nameless dread, the young mother shook her husband awake, and together they frantically searched their home to no avail.

Stalks The Cold Night

It was a gigantic creature of enormous strength and size, composed entirely of ice. However, some of the old tales say that inside the creature's ice-enshrouded body was a normal, human body that wore the frozen corpus as a shell. These wicked creatures stalked hunters in the night and regularly made meals of anyone unfortunate enough to meet them.

They woke their neighbors and formed a search party, desperate to find the missing child. At last, tracks which could only belong to the couple's baby were found in the snow leading towards the lake.

The search party raced on for a short distance but stopped short when they discovered the baby's cradleboard smashed to pieces. However, the tracks continued in the same direction towards the manido dwelling. Perplexed, the villagers noted with trepidation that the baby's tracks had changed to become larger, deeper and stranger. Though no one said it, all members of the search party knew that the baby had become a Wendigo.

Perhaps the baby had always been a Wendigo. Or perhaps the Wendigo's evil spirit had seized the baby's tiny body in a dream. Whatever the case, the young couple's baby was now a monster of the worst kind.

Some of the villagers fled back to their homes in terror, but the stoutest and bravest of the search party stayed the course. They were determined to aid the manido if they could or die bravely in the attempt. Unbeknownst to them, and even to the Wendigo itself, was the fact that Manidogizik was not alone in his dwelling by the lake. For many years, the Little People had served as his powerful guardians. These Little People were masters of the natural world; even common items such as sticks or stones could become deadly weapons in their hands. An old, dry stick could become a fiery missile, and a smooth rock could become a bolt of lightning.

As the Wendigo stalked closer to the manido's dwelling, the Little People felt the ground rumble beneath its heavy steps. They raced out to meet this fearsome monster, and a battle soon erupted between these two supernatural beings. The night sky was brightened and filled with the sounds of their raging conflict.

To the villagers in the distance, it appeared as if lightning and fire had waged war upon a mountain of ice. Thunder crackled in the air, and a primal scream, so loud and fierce that it could have shriven the very stones themselves, echoed in the night.

Then, as quickly as it had all begun, the night became suddenly dark and silent once more. Cautiously, the villagers crept towards the lake. To their surprise, they found the Wendigo sprawled upon the ground, dead. The manido stood nearby, leaning heavily upon a tree. His eyes were downcast, as he was lost in deep thought.

At last, he opened his eyes and spoke gravely to the villagers, instructing them to build a bonfire. Under the manido's guidance, the villagers then melted the Wendigo's massive body. When the ice had thawed, all that remained was the broken, lifeless body of the young couple's baby. The young mother wept profusely, but the manido grimly stated that if the Wendigo had not been slain, the foul creature likely would have eaten them all.

Fortunately for Man, not every fiend of the old world was a giant paradigm of insatiable evil. Some merely enjoyed giving people a good fright. One such creature was the Kashehotapolo of Choctaw folklore. This diminutive creature resembled a shriveled, old man with a grotesque face. It also possessed eyes that glowed like the embers of a waning fire. His lower extremities were like those of a deer, complete with sharp, cloven hooves.

The Kashehotapolo lived in dark swamps and thick forests, far away from the doings of men. However, solitary hunters would, at times, enter the Kashehotapolo's territory unknowingly while in search of game. The mischievous Kashehotapolo would then quietly sneak behind the human intruder and scream in a terrifying voice. Content with scaring the wits out of the hunter, the Kashehotapolo would then race away into the dim forest, laughing wildly all the while.

Most monsters, such as the Tlanuwa of Cherokee legend, preyed mercilessly upon mortals. These giant hawks built their nests high above on the formidable peaks of the Smoky Mountains. As birds of prey, they circled villages and settlements on the lookout for the young, the infirm, or the unwary. Like a falling star spiraling from the heavens above, the Tlanuwa would swoop down upon their human prey and carry them off with their sharp, cruel talons. The captured were not seen again.

Another horror to victimize the Cherokee in ages past was the Great Worm of the Smoky Mountains. Unlike most monsters, this creature relied heavily upon camouflage and guile to elude detection and to capture its favorite prey: women. This giant, worm-like creature had markings and appendages that resembled rough tree bark and branches. It was the monster's habit to stand upright and stock still, fooling everyone into believing that it was nothing more than an old, gnarled tree.

When the Cherokee men-folk left camp for the daily hunt, this vile creature would sneak into the village and silently murder and consume a defenseless woman. The creature would leave nothing behind but gory remains and torn clothing. For months, the Cherokee were baffled, and they vainly sought to find the perpetrator of these gruesome deeds, but to no avail.

Eventually, a solitary hunter, who had lost his wife to the Great Worm, saw the creature for what it truly was and devised a cunning plan. He advised the villagers to dig a large trench and to fill it with dry wood and pine cones.

Large stones, roughly shaped like women, were placed at the pit's edge. When all was ready, the dry wood in the pit was set ablaze. The flickering flames made the stones' shadows dance and wave so that from a distance it appeared that a group of Cherokee women danced at the rim of the trench.

The Great Worm was fooled by the ruse and crept close. It silently coiled itself to strike, intending to snatch a Cherokee woman by surprise. Instead, it was the worm that was taken aback, when it realized too late that the dancing women were nothing more than stones. The worm lost its balance and fell into the fire. Sparks and flame shot high into the sky, and the worm screamed. The monster's efforts to escape the blazing inferno were futile as the Cherokee, with clubs and spears, beat the creature back into the roaring flames. For most of the night, they watched with grim satisfaction as the worm thrashed and flailed in the fire. Finally, the creature died, and its body was soon consumed by the purifying flames. Never again would this denizen of the dark trouble the Cherokee. Yet, it seemed that another evil would always fill the void, and Man would receive very little respite from the growing darkness that surrounded him.

Winged Terror

These giant hawks built their nests high above on the formidable peaks of the Smoky Mountains. As birds of prey, they circled villages and settlements on the lookout for the young, the infirm, or the unwary.

It Comes For You

Another horror to victimize the Cherokee in ages past was the Great Worm of the Smoky Mountains. Unlike most monsters, this creature relied heavily upon camouflage and guile to elude detection and to capture its favorite prey: women.

Haunts The Clouds

These creatures were known as Big Heads, and that is exactly what they appeared to be, except for the disconcerting fact that they possessed no bodies. However, they did possess two large paws with razor sharp talons, which they used to tear human flesh.

For the tribes of the Iroquois Confederacy, thunderstorms were once feared, not only for their destructive winds and fatal lightning strikes, but also for the fearsome creatures said to have traveled within these chaotic tempests. These creatures were known as Big Heads, and that is exactly what they appeared to be, except for the disconcerting fact that they possessed no bodies. However, they did possess two large paws with razor sharp talons, which they used to tear human flesh. Their eyes were blood red, and their mouths were huge, gaping maws filled with rows of sharp, broken teeth. Fortunately, Big Heads, for all their ferocity, were not very smart. Many could be tricked or eluded by the quick-witted. However, in the deep, dark forests or secluded valleys they were rightly feared.

The Maidu of California feared a similar creature once said to have roamed the wilds in search of human prey. This creature was known by the tribes of the area as the Cannibal Head. The old tales say that, long ago, an evil man well-versed in the black arts accidentally injured himself while hunting. He licked the wound and enjoyed the taste of warm blood so much that he devoured his own body. Sustained by dark magic and human flesh, this monster haunted the foothills and forest of central California, forever seeking to slake his insatiable thirst for human blood.

Another creature of nightmares believed to have preyed upon the early Cherokee was the insidious monster known as the Iron-Fingered Demon. This dark being was a shapeshifter and had the ability to impersonate man, woman, or child. When the sun sank below the horizon, the Iron-Fingered Demon would set out from its deep cave and enter a village disguised as an absent member of a household.

Once it had infiltrated a home, the evil shapeshifter would seek to be inconspicuous until all the house occupants went to bed. With its soft fingers, the creature would then massage and stroke the head of its victims while singing a soothing nighttime lullaby. Once the human victim was lulled into an enchanted sleep, the demon would use its incredibly sharp iron fingers to perforate the victim's trunk and remove the lungs and liver. The wound healed magically and almost instantaneously, without even leaving so much as a bruise or scratch. With its ill-gotten gains, the creature would then return to its mountain lair to enjoy its awful meal of pilfered human organs. As for the mortal victim of the Iron-Fingered Demon, he or she would go about everyday business as if nothing was amiss. However, as time progressed, the individual would grow weaker and weaker, eventually dying pitifully of consumption.

The Miwok people once believed that a perilous creature called the Ettati made its home in the limestone caverns of the Sierra Nevada. Some tales say that the Ettati was a giant, lizard-like creature. Other tales hold that the creature was a giant serpent of cold, constricting coils. Most tales agreed, however, that the Ettati was a carnivorous terror that had plagued the Miwok for well-nigh untold generations. Though most people knew to avoid the ancient limestone caverns, the young and rebellious sometimes forsook the wisdom of their elders in the name of adventure. Many braved the rough mountainous terrain just to explore the depths of the living Earth. For those lucky few, the trips to the caverns were uneventful. Perhaps they would see nothing more than shadows dancing among the long stalagmites above. Maybe they would hear nothing more than drops of water from the cavern ceiling fall to disturb the surface of some dark and cold subterranean pool.

Those unlucky enough to lose their way or to travel too deeply into the caves were destined to suffer a different fate. The gentle rustle above, thought to be bats stirring in their slumber, would grow closer and closer. All the while, the oppressive stench of the caverns would grow stronger and stronger. Suddenly, without warning, the Ettati would strike like lightning from the gloom, savagely dragging its victim deep into the Stygian darkness.

According to the lore of the Kwakiutl people, the verdant forests were home to many strange and mysterious spirits. One particular spirit to be avoided was the cadaverous being known as Bukwus. From a distance, the spirit appeared to be an ordinary, mortal man. A closer inspection would reveal a being whose tattered, yellow skin just barely clung to ragged bones. Eyes, glazed and pale, would stare lifelessly from deep sockets. Blue lips, stretched and peeled, revealed the rictus grin of the dead. This creature could at times mimic human voices or use its formidable magical abilities to ensnare people. However, it was the creature's ability to cast powerful spells of bewilderment and insanity that made this hideous spirit so greatly feared.

The demonic Nalusa Falaya of Choctaw lore was another evil creature of the dark able to infect humans with madness. This creature was about half the size of a human. At times, it could appear as a deformed, old man with beady eyes, pointed ears, and a long, sharp nose. Like many creatures of the old world, the Nalusa Falaya lived in and around inhospitable areas like swamps, bogs, and stagnate marshes. Hunters that strayed into the creature's abode were wise to carry tobacco or other holy items on their person, as these objects kept evil at bay. Otherwise, the Nalusa Falaya would creep close to the hunter and call out the hunter's name. The hunter would faint from fright upon turning and seeing the wicked little creature laughing in the shadows. While unconscious, the diminutive monster would then implant a small thorn, imbued with dark power, into the hand or foot of the senseless hunter. The hunter, upon waking, would remember little. Henceforth, he would never be the same again. He would become an evil man who would inflict pain and misery onto his neighbors. In the worst cases, an individual so infected by the Nalusa Falaya would lose all sense of right and wrong, becoming completely insane.

The Tsimshian, Haida, and Tlingit of the Northwest acknowledged the presence of many spirits in the natural world. Of the multitude of supernatural beings to inhabit the shores and coastlines, the most feared and respected were the Land Otter People. These beings were shapeshifters, and they were able to assume the form of either man or otter. These Land Otter People often haunted the beaches and waterways, ever on the lookout for capsized canoes. In the guise of humans, they would aide drowning victims and take them to their lands. There, they attempted to feed the mortals fish and seaweed. Those who accepted the meal were transformed into Land Otter People themselves and would be forever estranged from the ways of mortal men. Some of the Otter People not only had the power to rob mortals of their humanity but even exercised power over the dead. The Land Otter Man of Tlingit tales, known as Kuskdaka, often walked the lonely coastline searching for the lost souls of the drowned. He stole these wayward spirits and brought them into a state of being known as Koosh-da-ka, transforming them into Land Otter Beings, forever bound to his ancient will.

Aside from robbing humans of their humanity, the Land Otter People also had the power to cause terrible inflictions, such as open sores and boils, upon unwary mortals. These dark feats were accomplished by the use of magically charged shells found in the great ocean depths. The Land Otter People also possessed powerful arrows made of spider crab shells. Each arrow was capable of causing mishaps and unfortunate accidents in the everyday lives of humans.

Worse yet were the Land Otter People's ability to rob humans of their senses. In Haida lore, such people afflicted by the Land Otter People were known as Gagixit or Wild Men. The shape-changing Otter People would sometimes transform into insects and crawl into the mouths, ears, noses, or any other orifices of sleeping hunters. The bewitched hunter would then be rendered senseless or foolish for the rest of his days, or worse: the hunter would lose all sense of reality and become completely mad.

Some monsters of the dark were especially feared by adults, because they solely preyed upon their most cherished possessions: their children. Nuwa parents told tales of the dreaded Haaka-painizi. This dark being sometimes wore the aspect of a giant grasshopper. In this form, he hunted the wide fields and valleys for unattended children. With his magical songs of binding, he could leave children immobile and catatonic. In such a state, the children could do little to fight back or run. Haaka-painizi would then scoop the children up in his sack. The children were never to be seen again.

Still worse were those dark beings who could overpower even the strongest of warriors with their wicked guile and cunning. The Deer Woman, a powerful spirit of the night who once haunted the Great Plains, was such a being. She was said to have the power to steal men's souls, along with their sanity.

This powerful entity also had the ability to assume the form of a young, attractive woman possessing an otherworldly beauty. With this disguise, she would frequent Pow Wows, ceremonies and other large gatherings, where there were sure to be large crowds of men. With her bewitching beauty, she would easily attract a young suitor and lead him away from the event.

Once alone, she would embrace her would-be lover with strength and power that belied her size. Her attractive guise would fade away, and the mortal man would find himself entangled in the clutches of a hideous, old hag that bore antlers on her gray crown and had cloven hooves instead of feet. The mortal victim would scream and struggle, but it would avail him naught, and the perilous Deer Woman would slowly take away her victim's years. In other words, the Deer Woman would steal a man's vitality and essence, thereby increasing her foul lifespan by a number of years. Her dark hunger sated, she would then release her hapless quarry and return to her cave before the sun came up. Her victim would remember very little of the experience.

Deceiver

One particular spirit to be avoided was the cadaverous being known as Bukwus. From a distance, the spirit appeared to be an ordinary, mortal man. A closer inspection would reveal a being whose tattered, yellow skin just barely clung to ragged bones. Eyes, glazed and pale, would stare lifelessly from deep sockets.

In The Shadows

The demonic Nalusa Falaya of Choctaw lore was another evil creature of the dark able to infect humans with madness. This creature was about half the size of a human. At times, it could appear as a deformed, old man with beady eyes, pointed ears, and a long, sharp nose.

Child Beware

This dark being sometimes wore the aspect of a giant grasshopper. In this form, he hunted the wide fields and valleys for unattended children.

Avoids The Sun

Still worse were those dark beings who could overpower even the strongest of warriors with their wicked guile and cunning. The Deer Woman, a powerful spirit of the night who once haunted the Great Plains, was such a being. She was said to have the power to steal men's souls, along with their sanity.

Like so many other mortals to have had dealings with the denizens of the dark, the Deer Woman's victim would forever be bewitched, forever rendered senseless and simple. In essence, he would be a living, breathing reminder of the dark powers that once held dominion over the night.

Chapter Five

Servants of Evil

CHAPTER FIVE

Servants of Evil

"Go forward, Faustus, in that famous art
Wherein all nature's treasury is contain'd.
Be thou on earth as Jove is in the sky,
Lord and commander of these elements.
-Doctor Faustus - Christopher Marlow

Whispered tales from the past speak of the Wise, men and women who were said to have understood and even controlled the unseen powers that were once abroad in that almost forgotten age. Those of the Wise who used their unique gifts for the betterment of mankind were known by many names. Some were called Wind Doctors and Listening Women. Others were known as Hataalii, Didanawisgi, or Midewinini. These wise healers, advisors, doctors, and seers were the receptacles of tribal history and forgotten lore. They were also the steadfast guardians of their people against the malevolent forces of the night.

Yet there were always those who misused their vast knowledge and power to attain selfish ends or even worse: there were those who dedicated their entire lives to the pursuit of evil. These wicked beings were known as witches.

In many ways, the practitioners of the dark arts were very similar to their benevolent counterparts, for they, too, had a deeper understanding of the natural order of the world. They also were able to manipulate the mighty elements and to commune with the ethereal spirits of the Earth. However, witches lacked the compassion and natural understanding of the Wise. For all their formidable might and knowledge, witches possessed no constructive purpose.

Instead, witches spent their days spreading sickness, misery, and death in their turbulent wake. Jealous, materialistic, and possessive beings, these witches often begrudged anyone who enjoyed success, whether it was of a personal or financial nature. So, it was not unheard of for wealthy individuals or families to become suddenly afflicted by disease, mental illness, droughts, floods, sterility, or even fires. Truly, witches were formidable enemies, but perhaps the single, most disturbing feature concerning them was the fact that they often kept their true natures hidden. Anyone, even a well-respected member of the community, could, in truth, be a witch of the worst kind. Not even the wise and benevolent medicine men and medicine women were above suspicion, because often it was hard to distinguish the good practitioners of medicine from the bad.

For the tribes of the Iroquois Confederacy, witchcraft was considered one of the most heinous and blasphemous acts that an individual could partake in. Yet, the attraction of power and the lure of forbidden knowledge were just too great for some people to resist. These ambitious individuals would often seek out the twilit groves and moonlit vales in the dead of night. It was the hope of these wayward souls to chance upon the periodic meetings of Hun-dat-nas, or witches. If successful in this mad endeavor, the would-be witch would then present himself or herself to the unholy gathering. If this individual was accepted and not killed outright by the witches, he or she would still have to prove worthiness by killing a close relative. Over time, the neophyte would then be taught how to curse a hated enemy from afar, how to bewilder the weak-minded, and how to create poisons for which there was no antidote. Most importantly, the would-be witch would learn the secrets to the art of shape-shifting.

The witches of Iroquois legend were master shapeshifters, able to transform into birds, beasts, or even inanimate objects, such as stones or tree limbs. When Hun-dat-nas needed to travel great distances or with urgency, they turned into ethereal glowing balls of light.

With such power at their disposal, it is not hard to imagine why the Iroquois tribes feared these malicious beings so greatly. However, their immense hatred of witches overrode their deep-seated fears of them. Suspect witches were usually killed outright or banished from Iroquois lands for all time.

The Alabama-Coushatta of the South also steeled their resolve when dealing with the supernatural powers of a witch. However, it often took great cunning and planning to defeat these masters of black magic.

In the days of yore, a great pestilence once devastated the people of the Alabama-Coushatta. It was a strange disease, in that it only struck those individuals who were wealthy or were members of the prominent families. The wise, old healers of the tribe were baffled. They could do very little to prevent the virulent sickness from taking hold. In time, many people began to suspect that the rising death toll was the work of an evil witch. However, the clan leaders were skeptical. A witch of such power had not been seen in Alabama-Coushatta lands for a very long time. The tribal leaders also knew that false accusations of witchcraft would sow distrust amongst tribal members. In time, such distrust could eventually lead to civil war. However, with the deaths of so many tribal members, the Alabama-Coushatta Miko was left with no choice but to act. In the dead of night, he called forth a secret council with the Alabama-Coushatta clan leaders. The primary purpose of this meeting was to determine the best way to identify and dispose of the witch.

Unfortunately, most clan leaders had no idea where to begin. Other clan leaders proposed absurd ideas that were impractical at best or dangerous at worst. In the end, it was the Miko, himself, who had conceived the best course of action.

Witches Gathering

The attraction of power and the lure of forbidden knowledge were just too great for some people to resist. These ambitious individuals would often seek out the twilit groves and moonlit vales in the dead of night. It was the hope of these wayward souls to chance upon the periodic meetings of Hun-dat-nas, or witches.

Witches In Flight

The witches of Iroquois legend were master shape-shifters, able to transform into birds, beasts, or even inanimate objects, such as stones or tree limbs. When Hun-dat-nas needed to travel great distances or with urgency, they turned into ethereal glowing balls of light.

Now, it must be noted that the current Miko was cast in a different mold than the previous chiefs who had come before him. The old Miko were men of action and had been mighty warriors in their day. The current Miko was more of an erudite, who had spent his youth listening at the feet of his elders. From the old tales, he knew that a witch had to amend his or her evil ways by bathing in the earth of the victim's grave. The Miko, armed with this knowledge, made plans for the clan leaders to attend the next funeral, but this time they would hide and wait for the witch to gather the unclean earth and follow his or her footprints.

Once the gathering of leaders had followed the veneficus home, they would know with certainty that the black magic user was indeed the source of all the tribe's ills. Several days after the clandestine meeting had occurred, another tribal member was afflicted with the same wasting sickness and soon died. The family of the deceased buried their loved one and stayed at the tribal cemetery for several long hours, until the sun sank beneath the western horizon. Stealthily hidden in the nearby brush waited the Miko and the clan leaders.

The night stretched on into the early hours of the morning, and still there was no sign of the witch. Many of the clan leaders grew restless, and some began to grumble that the entire outing had been a complete waste of time. However, as the moon hung low in the obsidian sky, a furtive figure slowly approached the cemetery. The men in hiding collectively held their breaths as the mysterious person glided to the fresh grave and began to gather the freshly dug earth. The hidden clan leaders could tell that the figure was a woman, yet they could not see her features, as she wore a shawl over her head.

They could also see that she walked with the aid of a tree branch. She used this branch for support when she bent down to scoop up the tainted earth. She then turned to leave but cast a backwards glance to the brush where the men hid.

Perhaps she felt eyes upon her, or maybe she heard the shallow breathing of one the clan leaders. In any event, she quickly left the cemetery and was soon lost to sight. The Miko and clan leaders sprang from the bushes and raced to the fresh grave to follow the witch's footprints. To their surprise and anger, they discovered that the witch had brushed away her footprints with the tree branch that she had used for support. Outside of the cemetery, the witch's footprints mingled with the footprints of all the other funeral attendees, and there was now no way to follow the witch to her dark abode. The tribal leaders now understood that, not only was this sorceress a powerful practitioner of the dark arts, but she was cunning as well. However, the Miko was a clever man, too. After some thought, he decided to make a few fundamental changes to his strategy.

Several weeks later, another prominent member of the tribe became a victim to the wasting sickness. As before, the Miko and the other headmen attended the funeral. Again, they lay in wait for the witch. However, this time, the Miko and his men took tree branches and erased all of the footprints around the grave. For good measure, they also left a ring of sand around the entire cemetery.

In the dead of night, a shrouded figure approached the cemetery. It was the witch, and, as before, she scooped down and gathered earth from the fresh grave. Once she had finished her dark deed, she then erased her footprints with a tree branch and disappeared into the trees. The Miko and the clan leaders raced to the strip of sand that they had placed around the cemetery.

And Lo! The Miko's plan had worked! In the sand lay the small footprints of the sorceress. Without a moment to spare, the tribal leaders quickly followed the footprints to the home of an old woman who lived alone in the dark forest. They stealthily approached the lodge, ready for anything, but found no one inside. The tribal leaders carefully surrounded the home and spied the old woman behind the lodge, bathing in dirt from the grave. In a voice that croaked with malevolence, she began to sing a song that caused the men's hair to stand on edge.

> "Listen! Now I have come to step over your soul.
> Your spittle I have put at rest under the earth.
> Your soul I have put at rest under the earth.
> I have come to cover you over with the black rock.
> Toward the black coffin in the Darkening Land your path shall
> Stretch out.
> So shall it be for you.
> The clay of the upland has come to cover you."

Before the sorceress could finish her terrible song of power, the tribal leaders sprang upon the dark being and killed her with their blessed knives. Her body was burned to ash and scattered by the four winds. From that day forth, the Alabama-Coushatta were never again troubled by the power of witchcraft, and they lived in peace for many long years.

Navajo witches, not to be confused with Skinwalkers, were known as Baenazeen. These particular witches practiced an evil and filthy type of sorcery known as the "Frenzy Way." Most suspected practitioners of this forbidden art were thought to be aged men and women who were childless or who had lost spouses under mysterious circumstances. However, some tales say that age is not a factor and that even the young could be practitioners of this black art. Most tales agree that Baenazeen, like their Iroquois counterparts, only used their vast knowledge for wicked deeds.

To accomplish their evil ends, it was said that these witches visited graveyards and cemeteries to search for fresh graves. The Baenazeen would disturb the silent repose of the dead by desecrating the gravesite in order to gather shinbones, which were used for arrows. They also cut off the fingers and toes of the dead in order to gather the skin whorls, which were an essential ingredient for their noxious poisons. Diné witches especially valued the flesh of deceased infants, which they used to create their greatest and most horrific weapon, corpse powder. By simply touching a victim with this powerful concoction, a witch could paralyze an individual for an indefinite amount of time. However, corpse powder blown into the face of a victim produced fatal results. The victim's tongue would turn black, while they suffered from violent convulsions and spasms. Finally, the victim of the witch would die a painfully long and agonizing death.

The blasphemous acts of these witches were a complete inversion of the "Blessing Way" practiced by healers. Baenazeen often traveled the lands at night, desecrating holy places or cursing those who had gained these witches' dire interest.

However, it was believed that if a witch was caught in the act of his or her practice, or if a witch's identity was discovered and made known, then it was the witch who would experience cosmic retribution by suffering the same maladies and afflictions of his or her intended victim. Sometimes, the wicked doings of a witch would be cut short by the members of the Navajo community themselves. After marshaling their courage, tribal members would seize, blindfold, and bind a suspected witch. Once confined and secured, the witch's victims were then expected to fully recover. The Baenazeen would then languish and wither away within a span of a year.

Witches also loomed large in the legends and folklore of the Tlingit tribes of the Northwest coast. Tlingit witches practiced a form of sorcery very similar to that practiced by Navajo witches. They, too, visited graveyards to harm their victims through malignant, magical practices. Often, the witch, called a Naak'w s'aati, would gather the personal articles of an individual, such as fingernail clippings, hair clippings, or garments. With these personal items in hand, a witch would then bury the articles in a fresh grave. Over time, as the dead body in the grave decomposed, the witch's victim would then become deathly ill. Without the intervention of a powerful Ixht', or wise man, the bewitched individual stood little hope of recovery.

It was also said, according to Tlingit folklore, that witches possessed the unnerving ability of flight. With this unnatural gift, a Naak'w s'aati sometimes flew to the rooftops of villagers and listened at the smoke holes while the dwellers inside unknowingly divulged embarrassing or damaging gossip. The witch would then blackmail the loose-tongued speakers mercilessly, often charging exorbitant prices for their silence.

It is also interesting to note that, while most Tlingit witches delved into the dark arts of their own volition, some were forced into this evil practice against their will. Legends hold that a person may be coerced into witchcraft by the enchantments and machinations of another more powerful witch. To be cured of this spiritual malady, a reluctant Naak'w s'aati had to seek out one who was more versed in the black arts than themselves.

This stronger witch would then proceed to open the afflicted individual's covers and remove the infectious evil blighting that person's soul. Tlingit folklore stated that a Naak'w s'aati had eight covers or folds of skin inside his or her body. Once the malignancy was removed from the covers of the afflicted, that individual would no longer be considered a witch. All thoughts and urges to practice evil would be purged, and the one-time witch would then be allowed to live out his or her life in relative peace.

If a suspected Naak'w s'aati refused treatment or had caused an unbearable amount of mischief and mayhem, the community would overcome their fear and aversion of the witch and react drastically. Tribal members would capture and then imprison the witch within a secluded dwelling. Deprived of food and water, the witch usually confessed to his or her sins and removed any and all curses upon his or her victims. Afterwards, exile was the prescribed punishment for the witch. In some extreme cases, the accused witch was executed by a family member or by one of the many warrior societies.

The Sorcerer

Navajo witches, not to be confused with Skinwalkers, were known as Baenazeen. These particular witches practiced an evil and filthy type of sorcery known as the "Frenzy Way."

Perhaps the most revolting of all of the witches of the old world were those who had once plagued the Creek nation. These creatures were considered most unholy and unclean, not only because of their evil deeds, but also for their disgusting habits and hygiene. These witches, known as Stegeny, were adept shapeshifters and were able to assume the form and likeness of almost any animal. Most often, they took on the dreaded shape and semblance of a great owl, an omen of ill portents for many tribes. To transform into the likeness of an animal, the Stegeny had to remove its viscera. The enchanter accomplished this by vomiting up its organs. These witches were extremely careful with their organs, and they took great pains to hide them well.

If a Creek hunter chanced upon the Stegeny's foul cache of organs, the hunter would often destroy them with fire. The witch would then be trapped in the shape and likeness of an owl for the rest of its unnatural days. Creek witches, however, were willing to risk such damnation for the sake of spreading evil and misery.

Stegeny often targeted the very young or the elderly, since they were considered easier prey. With the aid of special maledictions and an enchanted reed blow gun, the Stegeny could shoot blood clots into the legs of children. These blood clots had a crippling effect on young ones and often caused deformities. These witches were also believed to be the cause of any bad luck or illness that might happen to plague a Creek family.

Like many other witches of Native American lore, Stegeny kept their real identities hidden. Most lived quiet, normal lives and took part in the daily responsibilities and activities of the community. Some held positions of high honor and prestige. Even their outward appearance could be deceptive. It was believed that most Stegeny were elderly and decrepit men and women, seemingly incapable of harming anyone, but this was just a clever ruse. When the curtain of night fell upon the land, the seemingly enfeebled Stegeny would steal out into the darkness to spread pain and misery amongst the Creek community.

There were ways to recognize or even stymie the evil activities of these malicious witches. While Stegeny were masters in the art of shape-shifting, their illusions and transformations were not altogether flawless; they could be distinguished from real animals by their paw prints, which were irregular. Their movements, at times, could seem awkward or labored. There were even some members of the Wise who could see through their evil illusions and recognize these creatures for what they truly were. Even the observant listener would be able to distinguish between the forlorn cries of an actual owl and the crude imitations of Stegeny in owl form. It was said that the witch's cries would sound hollow and other worldly.

Despite the Stegeny's formidable and unholy powers, Creek lore says that these witches were easily frightened. Loud noises, such as the banging of pots and pans, or even yelling obscenities at them, could drive them away. Legend also says that tying the corner of a bed sheet into a knot while citing a prayer could "choke off" the Stegeny's voice, forcing the creature to flee into the night.

A truly brave soul could even destroy the witch altogether or, if the individual desired, steal the witch's power for their own ends. To accomplish this daunting task, a person had to put on their clothing backwards and wear their shoes on the opposite feet. In the black of the night, an individual would then have to walk outdoors backwards, directly to the place where the Stegeny lurked in owl form.

Transformation

These witches, known as Stegeny, were adept shape-shifters and were able to assume the form and likeness of almost any animal. Most often, they took on the dreaded shape and semblance of a great owl, an omen of ill portents for many tribes.

With a flint lighter or torch, the individual would then have to flash the fire into the face of the witch. The stunned witch would then be compelled to transform back into a human. Identity revealed, bereft of magical power, and completely helpless, the wily Stegeny would seek to bribe its captor with promises of riches or with dark knowledge. In other words, the witch offered to teach his or her captor the wicked ways of the Stegeny.

If the captor were just, he or she would either kill the witch outright or broadcast the witch's true identity to the public. Once the witch's identity was known, the General Council would then take measures to ensure that the witch never harmed another soul again. However, if the witch's captor lusted for unnatural power, then that individual would become an apprentice to the Stegeny. Very soon, there would be another foul witch gliding silently in the growing darkness.

The witches of the old world possessed many unnatural powers and strange abilities. Perhaps the most unnerving element about the practitioners of the dark arts was that not even death was a bar to their great hunger or vengeance. The Abenaki of the North once told unsettling tales of witches who refused to find peace after their deaths.

Once, in days long since passed, an old sorcerer of some note died of old age. In his long, unnatural life, he had been a vindictive and petty man. Any slight, real or imagined, was repaid ten-fold. In his day, he became feared by all throughout the Dawn Lands. When he passed away, there were no friends or colleagues to attend to his body. What few relatives he had finally wrapped him in blankets and placed his body in an old, gnarled tree deep in the heart of a black forest. In time, the forest became a place of dread. People saw strange things flitting in and out of the trees on moonlit nights. Hunters heard terrible sounds echoing from the burial grove. Eventually, men and women came to shun the unwholesome place altogether.

Several years later, a Mi'kmaq man and his wife were traveling through Abenaki lands on their way to the east. They did not know many people in those parts, so, instead of asking for a night's lodging, they decided to sleep under the stars. Looking for a good place to spend the night, they saw the old forest and set foot into that dark grove. When they entered, a chill took hold of the wife, and she questioned her husband about their night's stay. He merely laughed away his wife's fears and attributed them to superstition. The husband selected a large tree and built a small lean-to. He then prepared a fire and cooked their supper.

When their supper was over, the wife carefully studied their surroundings. It was winter, and most of the trees were bare. Dark and twisted branches seemed to stretch out and claw at the moon. Looking up, the wife saw dark shapes hanging amongst the trees. When she questioned her husband, he sleepily replied, "They're only the bodies of the deceased, but you shouldn't fear the dead. It's the living out there in the real world that we have to be mindful of. Come; it is time to sleep."

"We shouldn't be here. I think we had better leave now," replied the wife.

The husband merely laughed at his wife. He then rolled over onto his side and was soon fast asleep. The wife sat staring at the crackling fire and wished with all her might that she and her husband were anywhere but here. The night air had grown heavy, and it seemed to the wife that the eyes of the dark forest were upon her. At last, she, too, lay down beside the fire, but she could not sleep. As the night stretched on, the fire burned down to glowing embers. She gently prodded her husband, but he did not respond. She did not dare get up to gather more firewood in this dark place, so she wrapped herself in her blankets and shut her eyes.

It was not long after that she began to hear a gnawing sound. At first, she convinced herself that it was merely the old tree branches rubbing against each other in the wind- or maybe it was a small animal gnawing on the bones of one of the dead. The wife stayed awake the entire time and quietly listened to the strange grating sound that seemed to last for hours. Just when it seemed that she could take no more of the gnawing, it stopped. The wife breathed a sigh of relief and noted the brightening eastern sky as dawn slowly approached. The wife reached out to wake her husband, but he did not stir, so she let him be.

When the sun's golden rays had finally banished the shadows of the old forest, the wife roughly shook her husband by his shoulder. To her horror, he rolled onto his back with a face frozen in terror. He was dead, and the left side of his chest was a ruined mass of blood and viscera. The wife screamed and screamed and screamed. Half mad with terror, she then ran with all of her might to a lodge of the Abenaki. She tried to tell her story, but her words were incoherent and jumbled.

The Abenaki at first thought her mad, but they were gentle and tried their best to calm her nerves. Eventually, the wife was able to tell the gathering her harrowing tale, yet many would not believe her. The story was just too fantastic for them to find credible. However, a few of the old hunters remembered strange stories about the dark forest. They also recalled a name that was almost lost to legend, Skudakumooch, which means "ghost witch." With weapons in hand, a number of men went with the Mi'kmaq wife to the haunted grove. There, the troop found her husband lying under a burial tree. All could see that his heart was gone. The shaken men then looked up and saw the body of the dead witch high above. The bravest men in their number climbed the burial tree and took the accursed body down. They then carefully removed the tattered blankets and robes that covered the body. To their shock and horror, they discovered that the mouth of the desiccated corpse was covered with fresh blood.

The men burned the witch's body in a large bonfire and, for good measure, they burned down the burial tree as well. From that day forth, the old forest was a little bit brighter and cleaner. Shadows no longer held unseen menace, and wholesome animals once again returned to the grove. As for the poor wife, none really knew what became of her. Some said that she returned home to the lands of the Mi'kmaq and remarried. It was even said that she lived out the rest of her days in relative peace. However, most of the old people knew that this story was a fairy tale. The elders believed that any dealings with a witch, living or dead, would always result in a lifetime of nightmares.

Cherokee myths and legend are rife with harrowing tales of ghoulish witches and other horrifying workers of evil. While these creatures were rightly feared by mortals, there was one amongst this unholy gathering that inspired more fear and dread than any other. Even other practitioners of the dark arts feared this powerful being that had once preyed upon the weak and weary. This creature, known as the Ka'lanu Ahkyeli'ski, or Raven Mocker, was considered the worst kind of witch imaginable.

Like other witches, Raven Mockers hid within the tribal communities. For the most part, they appeared to be incredibly ancient men and women. This was only a clever facade. In truth, these witches were invisible but wore a costume of skin and flesh to avoid detection. With outstretched arms, these foul creatures would take to the night skies, flying high above in search of homes that housed the sick or dying. When these beings flew, sparks trailed behind them.

Once a home was identified, the witch would then descend with great speed toward the unfortunate dwelling. The witch's triumphant cry, which sounded like a raven's call, would then be heard echoing into the night. Such a cry was always an ill omen for the Cherokee, for it meant that someone would soon pass away. The Raven Mocker would then enter the home, unclad and invisible to the human eye, so that it may torment and terrorize the sick or dying.

After the Ka'lanu Ahkyeli'ski had tortured the ailing victim, the evil witch would seek to steal the life years of the terminally ill to increase its own long and foul life span. These beings accomplished this dastardly deed by magically taking and consuming a mortal victim's still-beating heart. However, certain Indian doctors and medicine-men could see and recognize these beings for what they were. If this came about, and the Raven Mocker's true form was perceived, then the creature would be stricken and die within a span of seven days. For this reason, medicine-men were often asked to sit with the dying, not only to provide comfort in their final hours, but also to protect them from the wicked doings of the Raven Mocker.

It was once believed by the Pomo, Konkow, and Maidu tribes of California that a great evil haunted the secluded mountain paths and lonely forest trails. The hunters and traders of the region were wise to travel in large groups, for only a fool would risk the chance of meeting the dreaded Bear Doctor alone in the darkling woods.

Bear Doctors were men and women who had gained dark, unnatural powers by donning magical bear costumes. These evil sorcerers had the unsettling ability to commune with wicked spirits and possessed the power to travel at tremendous speeds.

These witches won their dark skills through years of training under the tutelage of a former Bear Doctor. Sometimes, an individual could even purchase the bear costume and its magical abilities from another Bear Doctor. Usually, though, Bear Doctors would dig deep caves in the mountains, far away from habitation. In these dark dwellings, the Bear Doctor and his or her apprentices would construct their bear costumes. Through unholy rites, these witches would then imbue their regalia with the tremendous and savage power of the bear. With these ill-gained powers, Bear Doctors attacked and waylaid travelers for valuable items and goods. Some darker tales even hint that these witches may even have been eaters of the dead.

Raven Mocker

Like other witches, Raven Mockers hid within the tribal communities. For the most part, they appeared to be incredibly ancient men and women. This was only a clever facade. In truth, these witches were invisible but wore a costume of skin and flesh to avoid detection.

The Bear Doctor

Bear Doctors were men and women who had gained dark, unnatural powers by donning magical bear costumes. These evil sorcerers had the unsettling ability to commune with wicked spirits and possessed the power to travel at tremendous speeds.

As wicked as these beings were, some Bear Doctors did possess the ability to heal the sick. If an individual could pay a Bear Doctor's exorbitant fee, the witch might be inclined to aid the ill. However, more often than not, Bear Doctors were thought to be the source of many of the ills that plagued the northern tribes of California. These witches were master poisoners. Bear Doctors would spend months, from spring to winter, gathering poisonous plants and berries. These witches also collected bee and ant stingers, snake, spider, and scorpion venom, and a whole host of other deadly flora and fauna. Once these items were gathered, they were then placed into small bundles. The Bear Doctor, with the assistance of four apprentices, would then call upon the dark powers to administer the deadly concoction to the intended victim.

Although these witches were powerful and well-versed in the dark arts, there were ways to keep these evil shapeshifters at bay. Against these beings, prayer seemed to be the strongest defense. Medicine bundles, blessed by holy men, were often carried by hunters and warriors when they traveled abroad. Even weapons such as arrows and spears could be prayed over and blessed to make them more useful against the powerful Bear Doctor. Purification rituals performed in villages could cause these malevolent witches to avoid the entire region altogether. It is important to note that, as powerful as these beings were, they could still be killed with an arrow or spear to the neck.

Perhaps the most infamous witch of all Native American folklore and legend was the nefarious creature known as the Skinwalker. In truth, the name Skinwalker is a fairly new term. In the language of the Diné, these beings were known as Naagloshii or Yenaldoshi, which means "to travel on four legs." These Skinwalkers were master shapeshifters. They often took the shape of wolves or coyotes, but they could just as easily take the form of a dog, badger, antelope, or deer. Sometimes, they changed into something much worse, a cross between a wolf and man.

Many are the tales concerning these evil beings and their origins. Some legends hold that the Skinwalkers were gifts to the Navajo people from the Creator himself. These beings, capable of traveling at great speeds, served as messengers between different clans and encampments during times of war. Some stories say that Skinwalkers were especially valuable to the Navajo during their battles with the Ute and with the Spanish. However, with the introduction of the horse, Skinwalkers lost their purpose, and many began to use their God-given abilities for selfish ends. Other tales say that Adishgash or "The Witchery Way", the form of sorcery practiced by Skinwalkers, was first taught to Man long ago by Coyote, First Man, and First Woman.

To call the practices and ceremonies of the Witchery Way dark would be an understatement. This was the blackest and foulest form of evil magic imaginable. It made the dark rites and rituals practiced by all other witches seem celestial by comparison. In order to become a Skinwalker, an individual first had to be initiated into the dark order. Initiation always involved the blatant and unmitigated disregard for all cultural taboos. This usually culminated in the murder of a close relative or loved one by the would-be Skinwalker. After this heinous crime was committed, the neophyte would then be able to participate in all of the foul acts that these beings took part in. In dark caves, Skinwalkers made sand paintings of their intended victims. They would then urinate and defecate on these paintings to curse their victims with sickness or madness.

Skinwalker's Moon

In the language of the Diné, these beings were known as Naagloshii or Yenaldoshi, which means "to travel on four legs." These Skinwalkers were master shape-shifters. They often took the shape of wolves or coyotes, but they could just as easily take the form of a dog, badger, antelope, or deer. Sometimes, they changed into something much worse, a cross between a wolf and man.

They would also feast upon the flesh of badgers, lizards, dogs, coyotes, and many other animals considered unclean by the Navajo. An even worse trait was the fascination of the dead that these witches seemed to possess. Not only were these Skinwalkers grave robbers, stealing everything from jewelry to body parts, but they were also known for cannibalism and necrophilia.

In many ways, Skinwalkers were very similar to the Baenazeen, because they, too, made use of paralyzing poisons and concoctions made from the ground flesh and bones of human remains. It was believed that Skinwalkers climbed to the rooftops of Hogans and poured these foul potions down the smoke holes to sicken entire families. However, the main weapon of terror for the Skinwalker was the bone pellet, or bone bead, made from the shinbones of a corpse. The witch would attempt to either shoot or insert the bone bead into a victim's body, thereby stealing that person's vitality and sentencing the afflicted individual to a long and wasting death called Ghost-sickness.

Despite the Skinwalker's enormous powers and shape-shifting abilities, they, too, could be kept at bay by the Wise and by the knowledgeable. Corn pollen placed at the threshold or entrance would keep these witches from entering a Hogan. Certain herbs and plants could not only repel the Skinwalker but even offset the harmful effects of their poisons. Like the Stegeny of Creek folklore, the Skinwalker's animal disguise could be distinguished from a real animal by its movement and actions. A tell-tale sign was the Skinwalker's inability to keep its ears and tail still. While in animal form, Skinwalkers could be killed or injured if an individual had strong faith and dauntless courage. Sometimes, a wound was all that was needed to stymie these witches. A Skinwalker wounded in animal form would bear the same injury even upon returning to human form. Like the Bear Doctor of Pomo legends, the Skinwalker must be shot or stabbed in the neck while in animal form for the wound to be fatal.

Perhaps the best way to vanquish a Skinwalker was to spread the witch's true identity across the countryside. If a Skinwalker's actual name were made known to the public, the witch would soon die in a few short months, and a wicked being would be banished from the world of men for all time.

The powers of the old dark were seemingly overwhelming, but, despite the malevolent might of the monsters of old, not even they could halt the ascent of Man. In the end, for good or ill, Man has been and will always be the master of his own fate.

Terminat hora diem, terminat auctor opus.

Acknowledgments

Gratitude

The author would like to thank and acknowledge all of the following contributing individuals and organizations for their critical contributions. Without your efforts, this book would not exist: Laughter Smith, Elliot Serawop, Darren Delaune, Shane Negonsott, Jesse Hart, Tom White, Cory Latson, The Battise Family, The Anadarko Public Library and staff, The El Reno Public Library and staff, The Tribal Library of the Confederated Tribes of Grand Ronde, Oregon, Lindsey Schell, Lola Cowling, Shawna Bridgman

I would also like to thank the love of my life, Kelly, for standing beside me throughout the writing of this book. The research, editing, reading, sketching, and painting required to create this work was heavy. I don't think that I could have done it without you there to help shoulder the load. You've been my inspiration and motivation for continuing to improve my knowledge and move my career forward. Thanks for being there for me through thick and thin.

Reference Particularize

Bibliography

Barnouw, Victor, Wisconsin Chippewa Myths and Tales.
Madison: The University of Wisconsin Press, 1977

Beauchamp, W.M., Iroquois Notes. Journal of American Folklore.
July-Sept. 1882, pp 223-237

Blanchard, David, Who or What's a Witch? Iroquois Persons of Power.
American Indian Quarterly. Autumn-Winter 1982, pp 218-237

Burland, Cottie, North American Indian Mythology.
Feltham: Paul Hamlyn, 1968

Clark, E.E., Indian Legends of the Pacific Northwest.
Berkeley: University of California Press, 1998

Erodes, Richard and Ortiz, Alfonso, American Indian Myths and Legends.
New York: Viking Penguin Press, 1984

Erodes, Richard and Ortiz, Alfonso, American Indian Trickster Tales.
New York: Viking Penguin Press, 1998

Feldmann, Susan, The Storytelling Stone.
New York: Dell Publishing Co., Inc., 1965

Guiley, Ellen, Rosemary, The Encyclopedia of Vampires, Werewolves and Other Monsters. New York: Checkmark Books, 2005

Hazen-Hammond, Susan, Spider Woman's Web.
New York: The Berkeley Publishing Group, 1999

Holt, William, H., The First Americans.
New York: Holt, Rinehart, and Winston, 1981

Kelleher, Colm and Knapp, George, The Hunt For the Skinwalker.
New York: Pocket Books, 2005

Lankford, G.E., Southeastern Legends: Tales from the Natchez, Caddo, Biloxi, Chickasaw, and Other Nations. Arkansas: Little Rock Press, 1987

McHargue, Georgess, The Impossible People.
New York: Holt, Rinehart, and Winston, 1973

McNeese, Tim, Illustrated Guide to Native American Myths and Legends.
Stamford: Longmead Press, 1993

Niethammer, Carolyn, Daughters of the Earth.
New York: MacMillian Publishing Company, 1977

Owusu, Heike, Symbols of Native America.
New York: Sterling Publish Co., Inc., 1999

Wedel, Waldo, Prehistoric Man on the Great Plains.
Norman: University of Oklahoma Press, 1961

Wise, Lu Celia, Mini Myths and Legends of Oklahoma Indians.
Oklahoma City: Oklahoma State Dept. of Education, 1978

Wissler, Clark, Indians of the United States.
New York: Doubleday Company, 1940

About the Author

T. D. Hill (Wichita, Kiowa, and Pawnee) is a Native American artist, writer, motivational speaker, and fitness professional. He resides in Dayton, OH.

THE AGE OF MYTHS & LEGENDS

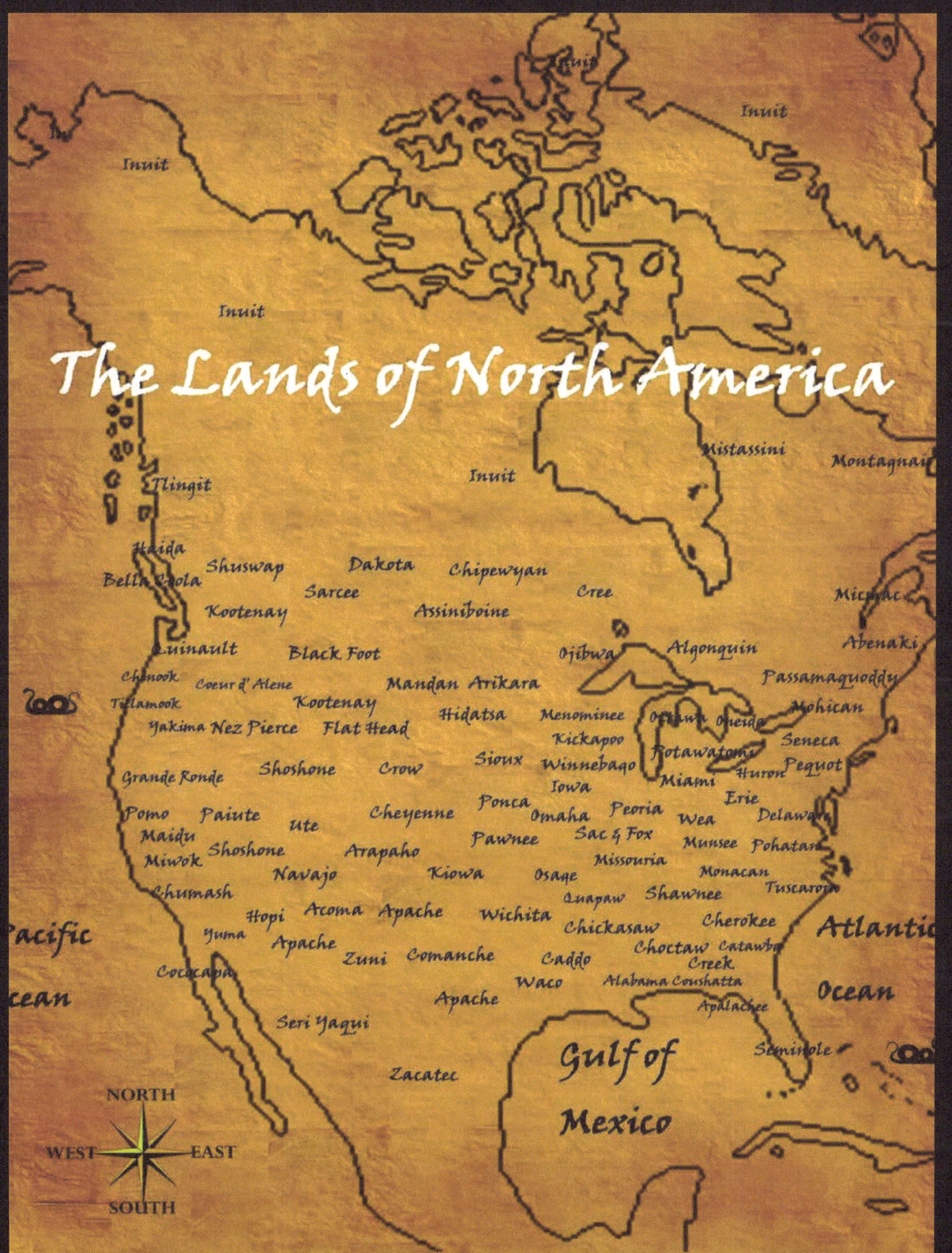

www.ingramcontent.com/pod-product-compliance
Lightning Source LLC
Chambersburg PA
CBHW040548010526
44110CB00047B/55